I0115582

Scriptural Rosary

CHARLES MICHAEL

Gifted Books and Media

Copyright

Scripture quotations marked GNT are from the Good News Translation in Today's English Version- Second Edition Copyright © 1992 by American Bible Society. Used by Permission.

Scripture quotations marked NRSVCE are from the New Revised Standard Version Bible: Catholic Edition, copyright © 1989, 1993 National Council of the Churches of Christ in the United States of America. Used by permission. All rights reserved worldwide.

Scripture quotations marked RSVCE are from The Revised Standard Version of the Bible: Catholic Edition, copyright © 1965, 1966 the Division of Christian Education of the National Council of the Churches of Christ in the United States of America. Used by permission. All rights reserved.

Scripture quotations marked NLT are taken from the *Holy Bible*, New Living Translation, copyright © 1996, 2004, 2015 by Tyndale House Foundation. Used by permission of Tyndale House Publishers, Inc., Carol Stream, Illinois 60188. All rights reserved.

Scripture quotations marked DRA are taken from the Douay-Rheims 1899 American Edition (Public domain)

Unless otherwise noted, scripture quotations are from Catholic Public Domain Version. Used by permission.

Compiled by Charles Michael

Printed in the United States of America

E-book ISBN: 978-1-947343-05-4
Paperback ISBN: 978-1-947343-04-7

Published by Jayclad Publishing LLC
www.giftedbookstore.com

Table of Contents

How to Pray the Scriptural Rosary

1. Make the Sign of the Cross

2. Say the "Apostles' Creed"

3. Say the "Our Father"

4. Say three "Hail Marys" for Faith, Hope, and Charity

5. Say the "Glory Be"

6. Announce the First Mystery

7. Say the "Our Father"

8. Read the Scripture verse before each Hail Mary (ten verses and ten "Hail Marys" per decade)

9. Say the "Glory Be"

10. Say the "O My Jesus" prayer

11. Announce the Next Mystery; and repeat the above steps (7-10).

12. Say the closing prayers (Hail Holy Queen, etc.)

13. Make the "Sign of the Cross"

The Joyful Mysteries

Decade 1 (The Annunciation)

Our Father...

In the sixth month, the Angel Gabriel was sent by God, to a city of Galilee named Nazareth, to a virgin betrothed to a man whose name was Joseph, of the house of David; and the name of the virgin was Mary. (Luk 1:26-27)
Hail Mary...

Upon entering, the Angel said to her: "Hail, full of grace. The Lord is with you. Blessed are you among women." (Luk 1:28)
Hail Mary...

When she had heard this, she was disturbed by his words, and she considered what kind of greeting this might be. (Luk 1:29)
Hail Mary...

The angel said to her, "Do not be afraid, Mary, for you have found favor with God." (Luk 1:30, NRSVCE)
Hail Mary...

Behold, you will conceive in your womb and bear a son, and you shall call his name Jesus. (Luk 1:31, RSVCE)
Hail Mary...

He will be great, and he will be called the Son of the Most High, and the Lord God will give him the throne of David his father. And he will reign in the house of Jacob for eternity. And his kingdom shall have no end. (Luk 1:32-33)
Hail Mary...

Mary said to the angel, "I am a virgin. How, then, can this be?" (Luk 1:34, GNT)
Hail Mary...

The angel said to her, "The Holy Spirit will come upon you, and the power of the Most High will overshadow you." (Luk 1:35, NRSVCE)
Hail Mary...

Therefore the child to be born will be holy; he will be called Son of God. (Luk 1:35, NRSVCE)
Hail Mary...

Then Mary said: "Behold, I am the handmaid of the Lord. Let it be done to me according to your word." And the Angel departed from her. (Luk 1:38)
Hail Mary...

Glory Be...

Decade 2 (The Visitation)

Our Father...

In those days, Mary, rising up, traveled quickly into the hill country, to a city of Judah. And she entered into the house of Zechariah, and she greeted Elizabeth. (Luk 1:39-40)
Hail Mary...

When Elizabeth heard the greeting of Mary, the baby leaped in her womb; and Elizabeth was filled with the Holy Spirit (Luk 1:41, RSVCE)
Hail Mary...

Elizabeth was filled with the Holy Spirit. And she cried out with a loud voice and said: "Blessed are you among women, and blessed is the fruit of your womb." (Luk 1:41-42)
Hail Mary...

Blessed are you who believed, for the things that were spoken to you by the Lord shall be accomplished. (Luk 1:45)
Hail Mary...

Mary said: "My soul magnifies the Lord." (Luk 1:46)
Hail Mary

My spirit leaps for joy in God my Savior. (Luk 1:47)
Hail Mary...

He has looked with favor on the humility of his handmaid. (Luk 1:48)
Hail Mary...

Behold, from this time, all generations shall call me blessed. (Luk 1:48)
Hail Mary...

He has stretched out his mighty arm and scattered the proud with all their plans. (Luk 1:51, GNT)
Hail Mary...

He has filled the hungry with good things, and the rich he has sent away empty. (Luk 1:53)
Hail Mary...

Glory Be...

Decade 3 (The Nativity)

Our Father...

While they were in Bethlehem, the time came for her to have her baby. (Luk 2:6)
Hail Mary...

She brought forth her firstborn son. And she wrapped him in swaddling clothes. (Luk 2:7)
Hail Mary...

She wrapped him in swaddling clothes and laid him in a manger, because there was no room for them at the inn. (Luk 2:7)
Hail Mary...

There were some shepherds in that part of the country who were spending the night in the fields, taking care of their flocks. An angel of the Lord appeared to them, and the glory of the Lord shone over them. They were terribly afraid. (Luk 2:8-9, GNT)
Hail Mary...

The angel said to them, "Be not afraid; for behold, I bring you good news of a great joy which will come to all the people." (Luk 2:10, RSVCE)
Hail Mary...

To you is born this day in the city of David a Savior, who is the Messiah, the Lord. (Luk 2:11, NRSVCE)
Hail Mary...

Glory to God in the highest heaven, and on earth peace among those whom he favors! (Luk 2:14, NRSVCE)
Hail Mary...

When the angels went away from them back into heaven, the shepherds said to one another, "Let's go to Bethlehem and see this thing that has happened, which the Lord has told us." (Luk 2:15, GNT)
Hail Mary...

When Jesus had been born in Bethlehem of Judah, in the days of king Herod, behold, Magi from the east arrived in Jerusalem. (Matt 2:1)
Hail Mary...

Entering the home, they found the boy with his mother Mary. And so, falling prostrate, they adored him. And opening their treasures, they offered him gifts: gold, frankincense, and myrrh. (Matt 2:11)
Hail Mary...

Glory Be...

Decade 4 (The Presentation)

Our Father...

The time came for Joseph and Mary to perform the ceremony of purification, as the Law of Moses commanded. So they took the child to Jerusalem to present him to the Lord. (Luk 2:22, GNT)
Hail Mary...

There was a man in Jerusalem, whose name was Simeon, and this man was righteous and devout, looking for the consolation of Israel, and the Holy Spirit was upon him. (Luk 2:25, RSVCE)
Hail Mary...

The Holy Spirit was with him and had assured him that he would not die before he had seen the Lord's promised Messiah. (Luk 2:25-26)
Hail Mary...

Guided by the Spirit, Simeon came into the temple; and when the parents brought in the child Jesus, to do for him what was customary under the law, Simeon took him in his arms and praised God. (Luk 2:27-28, NRSVCE)
Hail Mary...

Now you may dismiss your servant in peace, O Lord, according to your word. (Luk 2:29)
Hail Mary...

My eyes have seen your salvation, which you have prepared before the face of all peoples. (Luk 2:30-31)
Hail Mary...

The light of revelation to the nations and the glory of your people Israel. (Luk 2:32)
Hail Mary...

Simeon blessed them and said to Mary, his mother, "This child is chosen by God for the destruction and the salvation of many in Israel. He will be a sign from God which many people will speak against." (Luk 2:34, GNT)
Hail Mary...

After they had performed all things according to the law of the Lord, they returned to Galilee, to their city, Nazareth. (Luk 2:39)
Hail Mary...

The child grew, and he was strengthened with the fullness of wisdom. And the grace of God was in him. (Luk 2:40)
Hail Mary...

Glory Be...

Decade 5 (The Finding of the Child Jesus in the temple)

Our Father...

Every year the parents of Jesus went to Jerusalem for the Passover Festival. When Jesus was twelve years old, they went to the festival as usual. (Luk 2:41-42, GNT)
Hail Mary...

When the festival was over, they started back home, but the boy Jesus stayed in Jerusalem. His parents did not know this. (Luk 2:43, GNT)
Hail Mary...

They thought that he was with the group, so they traveled a whole day and then started looking for him among their relatives and friends. They did not find him, so they went back to Jerusalem looking for him. (Luk 2:43-45, GNT)
Hail Mary...

After three days they found him in the temple, sitting among the teachers, listening to them and asking them questions. (Luk 2:46, RSVCE)
Hail Mary...

All who listened to him were astonished over his prudence and his responses. (Luk 2:47)
Hail Mary...

Upon seeing him, they wondered. And his mother said to him: "Son, why have you acted this way toward us? Behold, your father and I were seeking you in sorrow." (Luk 2:48)
Hail Mary...

He answered them, "Why did you have to look for me? Didn't you know that I had to be in my Father's house?" (Luk 2:49, GNT)
Hail Mary...

They did not understand the word that he spoke to them. (Luk 2:50)
Hail Mary...

Then he went down with them and came to Nazareth, and was obedient to them. His mother treasured all these things in her heart. (Luk 2:51, NRSVCE)
Hail Mary...

Jesus advanced in wisdom, and in age, and in grace, with God and men. (Luk 2:52)
Hail Mary...

Glory Be...

The Sorrowful Mysteries

Decade 1 (The Agony in the Garden)

Our Father...

Then Jesus went with them to a garden, which is called Gethsemani. And he said to his disciples, "Sit down here, while I go there and pray." (Matt 26:36)
Hail Mary...

Taking with him Peter and the two sons of Zebedee, he began to be sorrowful and saddened. (Matt 26:37)
Hail Mary...

He said to them: "My soul is sorrowful, even unto death. Stay here and keep vigil with me." (Matt 26:38)
Hail Mary...

Going a little farther, he threw himself on the ground and prayed, "My Father, if it is possible, let this cup pass from me; yet not what I want but what you want." (Matt 26:39, NRSVCE)
Hail Mary...

Again, a second time, he went and prayed, saying, "My Father, if this chalice cannot pass away, unless I drink it, let your will be done." (Matt 26:42)
Hail Mary...

Again, he went and found them sleeping, for their eyes were heavy. (Matt 26:43)
Hail Mary...

Leaving them behind, again he went and prayed for the third time, saying the same words. (Matt 26:44)
Hail Mary...

Then he came to the disciples and said to them, "Are you still sleeping and taking your rest? See, the hour is at hand, and the Son of Man is betrayed into the hands of sinners." (Matt 26:45, NRSVCE)
Hail Mary...

Rise up; let us go. Behold, he who will betray me draws near. (Matt 26:46)
Hail Mary...

While he was still speaking, behold, Judas, one of the twelve, arrived, and with him was a large crowd with swords and clubs, sent from the leaders of the priests and the elders of the people. (Matt 26:47)
Hail Mary...

Glory Be...

Decade 2 (The Scourging at the Pillar)

Our Father...

Immediately in the morning, after the leaders of the priests had taken counsel with the elders and the scribes and the entire council, binding Jesus, they led him away and delivered him to Pilate. (Mrk 15:1-2)
Hail Mary...

Pilate went outside to them, and he said, "What accusation are you bringing against this man?" (Jn 18:29)
Hail Mary...

They responded and said to him, "If he were not an evil-doer, we would not have handed him over to you." (Jn 18:30)
Hail Mary...

Therefore, Pilate said to them, "Take him yourselves and judge him according to your own law." Then the Jews said to him, "It is not lawful for us to execute anyone." (Jn 18:31)
Hail Mary...

Then Pilate entered the praetorium again, and he called Jesus and said to him, "You are the king of the Jews?" (Jn 18:33)
Hail Mary...

Jesus responded, "Are you saying this of yourself, or have others spoken to you about me?" (Jn 18:34)
Hail Mary...

Pilate responded: "Am I a Jew? Your own nation and the high priests have handed you over to me. What have you done?" (Jn 18:35)
Hail Mary...

Jesus said, "My kingdom does not belong to this world; if my kingdom belonged to this world, my followers would fight to keep me from being handed over to the Jewish authorities. No, my kingdom does not belong here!" (Jn 18:36, GNT)
Hail Mary...

Pilate said to him, "You are a king, then?" Jesus answered, "You are saying that I am a king. For this I was born, and for this I came into the world: so that I may offer testimony to the truth. Everyone who is of the truth hears my voice." Pilate said to him, "What is truth?" And when he had said this, he went out again to the Jews, and he said to them, "I find no case against him. (Jn 18:37-38)
Hail Mary...

Pilate then took Jesus into custody and scourged him. (Jn 19:1)
Hail Mary...

Glory Be...

Decade 3 (The Crowning with Thorns)

Our Father...

Then the soldiers led him into the courtyard of the palace; and they called together the whole cohort. (Mrk 15:16, NRSVCE)
Hail Mary...

They put a purple robe on Jesus, made a crown out of thorny branches, and put it on his head. (Mrk 15:17, GNT)
Hail Mary...

They stripped him and put a scarlet robe on him. They wove thorn branches into a crown and put it on his head. (Matt 27:28-29, NLT)
Hail Mary...

They put a reed in his right hand and knelt before him and mocked him, saying, "Hail, King of the Jews!" (Matt 27:29, NRSVCE)
Hail Mary...

Spitting on him, they took the reed and struck his head. (Matt 27:30)
Hail Mary...

They began to salute him: "Hail, king of the Jews." (Mrk 15:18)
Hail Mary...

They struck his head with a reed, and they spit on him. And kneeling down, they reverenced him. (Mrk 15:19)
Hail Mary...

Then Pilate went outside again, and he said to them: "Behold, I am bringing him out to you, so that you may realize that I find no case against him." (Then Jesus went out, bearing the crown of thorns and the purple garment.) And he said to them, "Behold the man." (Jn 19:4-5)
Hail Mary...

But they were crying out: "Take him away! Take him away! Crucify him!" (Jn 19:15)
Hail Mary...

Pilate said to them, "Shall I crucify your king?" The high priests responded, "We have no king except Caesar." (Jn 19:15)
Hail Mary...

Glory Be…

Decade 4 (The Carrying of the Cross)

Our Father…

If anyone is willing to come after me: let him deny himself, and take up his cross every day, and follow me. (Luk 9:23)
Hail Mary...

Whoever will have saved his life, will lose it. Yet whoever will have lost his life for my sake, will save it. (Luk 9:24)
Hail Mary...

He then handed him over to them to be crucified. And they took Jesus and led him away. (Jn 19:16)
Hail Mary...

After they had mocked him, they stripped him of the purple, and they clothed him in his own garments. And they led him away, so that they might crucify him. (Mrk 15:20)
Hail Mary...

Carrying his own cross, he went forth to the place which is called Calvary, but in Hebrew it is called the Place of the Skull. (Jn 19:17)
Hail Mary...

14

They compelled a certain passerby, Simon the Cyrenian, who was arriving from the countryside, the father of Alexander and Rufus, to take up his cross. (Mrk 15:21)
Hail Mary...

A great number of the people followed him, and among them were women who were beating their breasts and wailing for him. (Luk 23:27, NRSVCE)
Hail Mary...

But Jesus, turning to them, said: "Daughters of Jerusalem, do not weep over me. Instead, weep over yourselves and over your children." (Luk 23:28)
Hail Mary...

Behold, the days will arrive in which they will say, 'Blessed are the barren, and the wombs that have not borne, and the breasts that have not nursed.' (Luk 23:29)
Hail Mary...

They led him through to the place called Golgotha, which means, 'the Place of Calvary.' And they gave him wine with myrrh to drink. But he did not accept it. (Mrk 15:22-23)
Hail Mary...

Glory Be...

Decade 5 (The Crucifixion)

Our Father...

When they arrived at the place that is called Calvary, they crucified him there, with the robbers, one to the right and the other to the left. (Luk 23:33)
Hail Mary...

Then Jesus said, "Father, forgive them; for they do not know what they are doing." And they cast lots to divide his clothing. (Luk 23:34, NRSVCE)
Hail Mary...

The passersby blasphemed him, shaking their heads and saying, "Ah, you who would destroy the temple of God, and in three days rebuild it, save yourself by descending from the cross." (Mrk 15:29-30)

15

Hail Mary...

One of those robbers who were hanging blasphemed him, saying, "If you are the Christ, save yourself and us." (Luk 23:39)
Hail Mary...

But the other responded by rebuking him, saying: "Do you have no fear of God, since you are under the same condemnation?" (Luk 23:40)
Hail Mary...

Jesus said to him, "Amen I say to you, this day you shall be with me in Paradise." (Luk 23:43)
Hail Mary...

Standing beside the cross of Jesus were his mother, and his mother's sister, and Mary of Cleophas, and Mary Magdalene. Therefore, when Jesus had seen his mother and the disciple whom he loved standing near, he said to his mother, "Woman, behold your son." (Jn 19:25-26)
Hail Mary...

It was now about noon, and darkness came over the whole land until three in the afternoon. (Luk 23:44, NRSVCE)
Hail Mary...

Then Jesus cried again with a loud voice and breathed his last. (Matt 27:50, NRSVCE)
Hail Mary...

Behold, the veil of the temple was torn into two parts, from top to bottom. And the earth was shaken, and the rocks were split apart. (Matt 27:51)
Hail Mary...

Glory Be…

The Glorious Mysteries

Decade 1 (The Resurrection of our Lord)

Our Father...

Therefore, you also, indeed, have sorrow now. But I will see you again, and your heart shall rejoice. And no one will take away your joy from you. (Jn 16:22)
Hail Mary...

On the first day of the week, at early dawn, they came to the tomb, taking the spices that they had prepared. (Luk 24:1, NRSVCE)
Hail Mary...

Behold, a great earthquake occurred. For an Angel of the Lord descended from heaven, and as he approached, he rolled back the stone and sat down on it. (Matt 28:2)
Hail Mary...

Then the Angel responded by saying to the women: "Do not be afraid. For I know that you are seeking Jesus, who was crucified. He is not here. For he has risen, just as he said. Come and see the place where the Lord was placed." (Matt 28:5-6)
Hail Mary...

He is not here, for he has risen. Recall how he spoke to you, when he was still in Galilee, saying: 'For the Son of man must be delivered into the hands of sinful men, and be crucified, and on the third day rise again.' (Luk 24:6-7)
Hail Mary...

Go quickly now, and tell his disciples, 'He has been raised from death, and now he is going to Galilee ahead of you; there you will see him!' Remember what I have told you. (Matt 28:7, GNT)
Hail Mary...

They went out of the tomb quickly, with fear and in great joy, running to announce it to his disciples. (Matt 28:8)
Hail Mary...

Suddenly Jesus met them and said, "Peace be with you." They came up to him, took hold of his feet, and worshiped him. (Matt 28:9, GNT)
Hail Mary...

Then Jesus said to them: "Do not be afraid. Go, announce it to my brothers, so that they may go to Galilee. There they shall see me." (Matt 28:10)
Hail Mary...

After his suffering he presented himself alive to them by many convincing proofs, appearing to them during forty days and speaking about the kingdom of God. (Acts 1:3, NRSVCE)
Hail Mary...

Glory Be...

Decade 2 (The Ascension)

Our Father...

Then he led them out as far as Bethania. And lifting up his hands, he blessed them. (Luk 24:50)
Hail Mary...

Jesus, drawing near, spoke to them, saying: "All authority has been given to me in heaven and on earth." (Matt 28:18)
Hail Mary...

Therefore, go forth and teach all nations, baptizing them in the name of the Father and of the Son and of the Holy Spirit. (Matt 28:19)
Hail Mary...

Teach them to obey everything I have commanded you. (Matt 28:20, GNT)
Hail Mary...

I will be with you always, to the end of the age. (Matt 28:20, GNT)
Hail Mary...

It happened that, while he was blessing them, he withdrew from them, and he was carried up into heaven. (Luk 24:51)
Hail Mary...

Indeed, the Lord Jesus, after he had spoken to them, was taken up into heaven, and he sits at the right hand of God. (Mrk 16:19)

Hail Mary...

They worshiped him, and returned to Jerusalem with great joy. (Luk 24:52, NRSVCE)
Hail Mary...

They were always in the temple, praising and blessing God. (Luk 24:53)
Hail Mary...

They went out and proclaimed the good news everywhere, while the Lord worked with them and confirmed the message by the signs that accompanied it. (Mrk 16:20, NRSVCE)
Hail Mary...Glory Be...

Decade 3 (The Coming of the Holy Spirit)

Our Father...

I am sending the Promise of my Father upon you. But you must stay in the city, until such time as you are clothed with power from on high. (Luk 24:49)
Hail Mary...

When they came together, he gave them this order: "Do not leave Jerusalem, but wait for the gift I told you about, the gift my Father promised. John baptized with water, but in a few days you will be baptized with the Holy Spirit." (Acts 1:4-5, GNT)
Hail Mary...

When they had entered the city, they went to the room upstairs where they were staying, Peter, and John, and James, and Andrew, Philip and Thomas, Bartholomew and Matthew, James son of Alphaeus, and Simon the Zealot, and Judas son of James. (Acts 1:13, NRSVCE)
Hail Mary...

When the days of Pentecost were completed, they were all together in the same place. And suddenly, there came a sound from heaven, like that of a wind approaching violently, and it filled the entire house where they were sitting. (Acts 2:1-2)
Hail Mary...

Divided tongues, as of fire, appeared among them, and a tongue rested on each of them. (Acts 2:3, NRSVCE)

19

Hail Mary...

They were all filled with the Holy Spirit and began to talk in other languages, as the Spirit enabled them to speak. (Acts 2:4, GNT)
Hail Mary...

When this sound occurred, the multitude came together and was confused in mind, because each one was listening to them speaking in his own language. (Acts 2:6)
Hail Mary...

Therefore, being exalted to the right hand of God, and having received from the Father the Promise of the Holy Spirit, he poured this out, just as you now see and hear. (Acts 2:33)
Hail Mary...

I will pour out my spirit upon all flesh, and your sons and your daughters will prophesy; your elders will dream dreams, and your youths will see visions. (Joel 2:28)
Hail Mary...

In those days I will pour out my spirit upon my servants and handmaids. And I will grant wonders in the sky and on earth: blood and fire and the vapor of smoke. (Joel 2:29-30)
Hail Mary...Glory Be...

Decade 4 (The Assumption of the Blessed Virgin Mary)

Our Father...

Then God's temple in heaven was opened, and the ark of his covenant was seen within his temple; and there were flashes of lightning, rumblings, peals of thunder, an earthquake, and heavy hail. (Rev 11:19, NRSVCE)
Hail Mary...

Great sign appeared in heaven: a woman clothed with the sun, and the moon was under her feet, and on her head was a crown of twelve stars. (Rev 12:1)
Hail Mary...

She was soon to give birth, and the pains and suffering of childbirth made her cry out. (Rev 12:2, GNT)
Hail Mary...

After the dragon saw that he had been thrown down to the earth, he pursued the woman who brought forth the male child. (Rev 12:13)
Hail Mary...

The woman was given the two wings of the great eagle, so that she could fly from the serpent into the wilderness, to her place where she is nourished for a time, and times, and half a time. (Rev 12:14, NRSVCE)
Hail Mary...

The dragon was angry at the woman. And so he went away to do battle with the remainder of her offspring, those who keep the commandments of God and who hold to the testimony of Jesus Christ. (Rev 12:17)
Hail Mary...

The prayer of one who humbles himself will pierce the clouds. And it will not be consoled until it draws near; and it will not withdraw until the Most High beholds. (Sir 35:21)
Hail Mary...

Be humbled under the powerful hand of God, so that he may exalt you in the time of visitation. (1 Pet 5:6)
Hail Mary...

God resists the proud, but gives grace to the humble. (Jas 4:6, GNT)
Hail Mary...

Turn to the Lord, all you humble people of the land, who obey his commands. Do what is right, and humble yourselves before the Lord. Perhaps you will escape punishment on the day when the Lord shows his anger. (Zeph 2:3, GNT)
Hail Mary... Glory Be...

Decade 5 (The Coronation of the Blessed Mother)

Our Father...

The Mighty One has done great things for me, and holy is his name. (Luk 1:49, NRSVCE)
Hail Mary...

The Most High God has blessed you more than any other woman on earth. How worthy of praise is the Lord God who created heaven and earth! (Judith 13:18, GNT)

Hail Mary...

All these were constantly devoting themselves to prayer, together with certain women, including Mary the mother of Jesus, as well as his brothers. (Acts 1:14, NRSVCE)
Hail Mary...

Through the heart of the mercy of our God, by which, descending from on high, he has visited us, to illuminate those who sit in darkness and in the shadow of death, and to direct our feet in the way of peace. (Luk 1:78-79)
Hail Mary...

It happened that, when he was saying these things, a certain woman from the crowd, lifting up her voice, said to him, "Blessed is the womb that bore you and the breasts that nursed you." (Luk 11:27)
Hail Mary...

My song will keep your fame alive forever, and everyone will praise you for all time to come. (Ps 45:17, GNT)
Hail Mary...

When Jesus had seen his mother and the disciple whom he loved standing near, he said to his mother, "Woman, behold your son." Next, he said to the disciple, "Behold your mother." And from that hour, the disciple accepted her as his own. (Jn 19:26-27)
Hail Mary...

Obedience is better than sacrifice. And to heed is greater than to offer the fat of rams. (1 Sam 15:22)
Hail Mary...

Blessed are those who preserve my ways. Listen to discipline, and become wise, and do not be willing to cast it aside. (Pro 8:32-33)
Hail Mary...

Whoever obeys me will not be put to shame, and those who work with me will not sin." (Sir 24:22, NRSVCE)

Hail Mary...Glory Be…

The Luminous Mysteries

Decade 1 (The Baptism of our Lord)

Our Father...

I baptize you with water for repentance, but he who will come after me is more powerful than me. I am not worthy to carry his shoes. He will baptize you with the fire of the Holy Spirit. (Matt 3:11)
Hail Mary...

This is he of whom I said, "After me comes a man who ranks ahead of me because he was before me." (Jn 1:30, NRSVCE)
Hail Mary...

I myself did not know him; but I came baptizing with water for this reason, that he might be revealed to Israel. (Jn 1:31, NRSVCE)
Hail Mary...

Jesus came from Galilee, to John at the Jordan, in order to be baptized by him. (Matt 3:13)
Hail Mary...

John tried to make him change his mind. "I ought to be baptized by you," John said, "and yet you have come to me!" (Matt 3:14, GNT)
Hail Mary...

Jesus answered him, "Let it be so for now. For in this way we shall do all that God requires." So John agreed. (Matt 3:15, GNT)
Hail Mary...

Jesus, having been baptized, ascended from the water immediately, and behold, the heavens were opened to him. And he saw the Spirit of God descending like a dove, and alighting on him. (Matt 3:16)
Hail Mary...

Behold, there was a voice from heaven, saying: "This is my beloved Son, in whom I am well pleased." (Matt 3:17)
Hail Mary...

John offered testimony, saying: "For I saw the Spirit descending from heaven like a dove; and he remained upon him." (Jn 1:32)
Hail Mary...

I did not know him. But he who sent me to baptize with water said to me: 'He over whom you will see the Spirit descending and remaining upon him, this is the one who baptizes with the Holy Spirit.' (Jn 1:33)
Hail Mary...

Glory Be...

Decade 2 (The Wedding at Cana)

Our Father...

On the third day, a wedding was held in Cana of Galilee, and the mother of Jesus was there. Now Jesus was also invited to the wedding, with his disciples. (Jn 2:1-2)
Hail Mary...

When the wine had given out, Jesus' mother said to him, "They are out of wine." (Jn 2:3, GNT)
Hail Mary...

Jesus said to her: "What is that to me and to you, woman? My hour has not yet arrived." (Jn 2:4)
Hail Mary...

His mother said to the servants, "Do whatever he tells you." (Jn 2:5)
Hail Mary...

The Jews have rules about ritual washing, and for this purpose six stone water jars were there, each one large enough to hold between twenty and thirty gallons. (Jn 2:6, GNT)
Hail Mary...

Jesus said to them, "Fill the water jars with water." And they filled them to the very top. (Jn 2:7)
Hail Mary...

Jesus said to them, "Now draw from it, and carry it to the chief steward of the feast." And they took it to him. (Jn 2:8)
Hail Mary...

When the chief steward had tasted the water made into wine, since he did not know where it was from, for only the servants who had drawn the water knew, the chief steward called the groom. (Jn 2:9)
Hail Mary...

24

And said to him, "Everyone serves the good wine first, and then the inferior wine after the guests have become drunk. But you have kept the good wine until now." (Jn 2:10, NRSVCE)
Hail Mary...

This was the beginning of the signs that Jesus accomplished in Cana of Galilee, and it manifested his glory, and his disciples believed in him. (Jn 2:11)
Hail Mary...

Glory Be...

Decade 3 (The Proclamation of the Kingdom)

Our Father...

The time has been fulfilled and the kingdom of God has drawn near. Repent and believe in the Gospel. (Mrk 1:15)
Hail Mary...

Jesus responded: "Amen, amen, I say to you, unless one has been reborn by water and the Holy Spirit, he is not able to enter into the kingdom of God." (Jn 3:5)
Hail Mary...

From that time, Jesus began to preach, and to say: "Repent. For the kingdom of heaven has drawn near." (Matt 4:17)
Hail Mary...

Jesus traveled throughout all of Galilee, teaching in their synagogues, and preaching the Gospel of the kingdom, and healing every sickness and every infirmity among the people. (Matt 4:23)
Hail Mary...

Going forth, preach, saying: 'For the kingdom of heaven has drawn near.' Cure the infirm, raise the dead, cleanse lepers, cast out demons. You have received freely, so give freely. (Matt 10:7-8)
Hail Mary...

Into whatever city you have entered and they have received you, eat what they set before you. And cure the sick who are in that place, and proclaim to them, 'The kingdom of God has drawn near to you.' (Luk 10:8-9)
Hail Mary...

This Good News about the Kingdom will be preached through all the world for a witness to all people; and then the end will come. (Matt 24:14, GNT)
Hail Mary...

It happened afterwards that he was making a journey through the cities and towns, preaching and evangelizing the kingdom of God. And the twelve were with him. (Luk 8:1)
Hail Mary...

When the crowd had realized this, they followed him. And he received them and spoke to them about the kingdom of God. And those who were in need of cures, he healed. (Luk 9:11)
Hail Mary...

Jesus traveled throughout all of the cities and towns, teaching in their synagogues, and preaching the Gospel of the kingdom, and healing every illness and every infirmity. (Matt 9:35)
Hail Mary...

Glory Be...

Decade 4 (The Transfiguration)

Our Father...

After six days, Jesus took Peter and James and his brother John, and he led them onto a lofty mountain separately. (Matt 17:1)
Hail Mary...

He was transfigured before them. And his face shined brightly like the sun. And his garments were made white like snow. (Matt 17:2)
Hail Mary...

Behold, there appeared to them Moses and Elijah, speaking with him. (Matt 17:3)
Hail Mary...

His clothes became dazzling white, such as no one on earth could bleach them. (Mrk 9:3, NRSVCE)
Hail Mary...

Peter responded by saying to Jesus: "Lord, it is good for us to be here.

If you are willing, let us make three tabernacles here, one for you, one for Moses, and one for Elijah." (Matt 17:4)
Hail Mary...

While he was still speaking, behold, a shining cloud overshadowed them. And behold, there was a voice from the cloud, saying: "This is my beloved Son, with whom I am well pleased. Listen to him." (Matt 17:5)
Hail Mary...

When the disciples heard the voice, they were so terrified that they threw themselves face downward on the ground. (Matt 17:6, GNT)
Hail Mary...

Jesus drew near and touched them. And he said to them, "Rise up and do not be afraid." (Matt 17:7)
Hail Mary...

Lifting up their eyes, they saw no one, except Jesus alone. (Matt 17:8)
Hail Mary...

As they were descending from the mountain, Jesus instructed them, saying, "Tell no one about the vision, until the Son of man has risen from the dead." (Matt 17:9)
Hail Mary...

Glory Be...

Decade 5 (The Institution of the Last Supper)

Our Father...

On the first day of Unleavened Bread, the disciples approached Jesus, saying, "Where do you want us to prepare for you to eat the Passover?" (Matt 26:17)
Hail Mary...

Jesus said, "Go into the city, to a certain one, and say to him: 'The Teacher said: My time is near. I am observing the Passover with you, along with my disciples.' "(Matt 26:18)
Hail Mary...

The disciples did just as Jesus appointed to them. And they prepared the Passover. (Matt 26:19)
Hail Mary...

When evening arrived, he sat at table with his twelve disciples. And while they were eating, he said: "Amen I say to you, that one of you is about to betray me." (Matt 26:20-21)
Hail Mary...

The disciples were very upset and began to ask him, one after the other, "Surely, Lord, you don't mean me?" Jesus answered, "One who dips his bread in the dish with me will betray me. (Matt 26:22-23, GNT)
Hail Mary...

Indeed, the Son of man goes, just as it has been written about him. But woe to that man by whom the Son of man will be betrayed. It would be better for that man if he had not been born. (Matt 26:24)
Hail Mary...

While they were eating the meal, Jesus took bread, and he blessed and broke and gave it to his disciples, and he said: "Take and eat. This is my body." (Matt 26:26)
Hail Mary...

Taking the chalice, he gave thanks. And he gave it to them, saying: "Drink from this, all of you." (Matt 26:27)
Hail Mary...

This is my blood of the covenant, which is poured out for many for the forgiveness of sins. (Matt 26:28, NRSVCE)
Hail Mary...

But I say to you, I will not drink again from this fruit of the vine, until that day when I will drink it new with you in the kingdom of my Father. (Matt 26:29)
Hail Mary...

Glory Be...

Prophecies about Jesus

Decade 1

Our Father...

Judah will hold the royal scepter, and his descendants will always rule. Nations will bring him tribute and bow in obedience before him. (Gen 49:10, GNT)
Hail Mary...

When your days will have been fulfilled, and you will sleep with your fathers, I will raise up your offspring after you, who will go forth from your loins, and I will make firm his kingdom. He himself shall build a house to my name. And I will establish the throne of his kingdom, even forever. (2 Sam 7:12-13)
Hail Mary...

The Lord himself will grant to you a sign. Behold, a virgin will conceive, and she will give birth to a son, and his name will be called Immanuel. (Is 7:14)
Hail Mary...

Israel was a child and I loved him; and out of Egypt I called my son. (Hos 11:1)
Hail Mary...

You, O Bethlehem of Ephrathah, who are one of the little clans of Judah, from you shall come forth for me one who is to rule in Israel, whose origin is from of old, from ancient days. (Mic 5:2, GNT)
Hail Mary...

I will put enmity between you and the woman, and between your offspring and hers; he will strike your head, and you will strike his heel. (Gen 3:15, NRSVCE)
Hail Mary...

I will open my mouth in a parable; I will utter dark sayings from of old. (Ps 78:2, NRSVCE)
Hail Mary...

He will become a sanctuary, a stone one strikes against; for both houses of Israel he will become a rock one stumbles over — a trap and a snare for the inhabitants of Jerusalem. (Is 8:14, NRSVCE)
Hail Mary...

In the earlier time, the land of Zebulun and the land of Naphtali were lifted up. But in the later time, the way of the sea beyond the Jordan, the Galilee of the Gentiles, was weighed down. The people who walked in darkness have seen a great light. A light has risen for the inhabitants of the region of the shadow of death. (Is 9:1-2)
Hail Mary...

A child is born to us! A son is given to us! And he will be our ruler. He will be called, "Wonderful Counselor," "Mighty God," "Eternal Father," "Prince of Peace." (Is 9:6, GNT)
Hail Mary...

Glory Be...

Decade 2

Our Father...

A day is coming when the new king from the royal line of David will be a symbol to the nations. They will gather in his royal city and give him honor. (Is 11:10, GNT)
Hail Mary...

The royal line of David is like a tree that has been cut down; but just as new branches sprout from a stump, so a new king will arise from among David's descendants. (Is 11:1, GNT)
Hail Mary...

Strengthen the weak hands, and make firm the feeble knees. Say to those who are of a fearful heart, "Be strong, do not fear! Here is your God. He will come with vengeance, with terrible recompense. He will come and save you." (Is 35:3-4, NRSVCE)
Hail Mary...

The voice of one crying out in the desert: "Prepare the way of the Lord! Make straight the paths of our God, in a solitary place. Every valley will be exalted, and every mountain and hill will be brought low. And the crooked will be straightened, and the uneven will become level ways." (Is 40:3-4)

30

Hail Mary...

Behold my servant, I will uphold him, my elect, with him my soul is well-pleased. I have sent my Spirit upon him. He will offer judgment to the nations. He will not cry out, and he will not show favoritism to anyone; neither will his voice be heard abroad. The bruised reed he will not break, and the smoldering wick he will not extinguish. He will lead forth judgment unto truth. He will not be saddened or troubled, until he establishes judgment on earth. (Is 42:1-4)
Hail Mary...

He will rise up like a tender plant in his sight, and like a root from the thirsty ground. There is no beautiful or stately appearance in him. For we looked upon him, and there was no aspect, such that we would desire him. (Is 53:2)
Hail Mary...

He is despised and the least among men, a man of sorrows who knows infirmity. And his countenance was hidden and despised. Because of this, we did not esteem him. (Is 53:3)
Hail Mary...

He endured the suffering that should have been ours, the pain that we should have borne. All the while we thought that his suffering was punishment sent by God. (Is 53:4, GNT)
Hail Mary...

He himself was wounded because of our iniquities. He was bruised because of our wickedness. The discipline of our peace was upon him. And by his wounds, we are healed. (Is 53:5)
Hail Mary...

We have all gone astray like sheep; each one has turned aside to his own way. And the Lord has placed all our iniquity upon him. (Is 53:6)
Hail Mary...

Glory Be...

Decade 3

Our Father...

He was oppressed, and he was afflicted, yet he did not open his mouth; like a lamb that is led to the slaughter, and like a sheep that

31

before its shearers is silent, so he did not open his mouth. (Is 53:7, NRSVCE)
Hail Mary...

I watched, therefore, in the vision of the night, and behold, with the clouds of heaven, one like a son of man arrived, and he approached all the way to the Ancient of days, and they presented him before him. And he gave him power, and honor, and the kingdom, and all peoples, tribes, and languages will serve him. His power is an eternal power, which will not be taken away, and his kingdom, one which will not be corrupted. (Dan 7:13-14)
Hail Mary...

Rejoice well, daughter of Zion, shout for joy, daughter of Jerusalem. Behold, your King will come to you: the Just One, the Savior. He is poor and riding upon a donkey, and upon a colt, the son of a donkey. (Zech 9:9)
Hail Mary...

They weighed for my wages thirty silver coins. And the Lord said to me: Cast it towards the statuary, the handsome price at which I have been valued by them. And I took the thirty silver coins, and I cast them into the house of the Lord, towards the statuary. (Zech 11:12-13)
Hail Mary...

Behold, I will send to you Elijah the prophet, before the arrival of the great and terrible day of the Lord. And he will turn the heart of the fathers to the sons, and the heart of the sons to their fathers. (Mal 4:5-6)
Hail Mary...

The life of the flesh is in the blood, and I have given it to you, so that you may atone with it upon the altar for your souls, and so that the blood may be for an expiation of the soul. (Lev 17:11)
Hail Mary...

I know that my Redeemer lives, and that at the last he will stand upon the earth. (Job 19:25, NRSVCE)
Hail Mary...

My God, my God, why have you abandoned me? I have cried desperately for help, but still it does not come. (Ps 22:1, GNT)

Hail Mary...

My mouth is dried up like a potsherd, and my tongue sticks to my jaws; you lay me in the dust of death. (Ps 22:15, NRSVCE)
Hail Mary...

For dogs are all around me; a company of evildoers encircles me. My hands and feet have shriveled; I can count all my bones. They stare and gloat over me. (Ps 22:16-17, NRSVCE)
Hail Mary...

Glory Be...

Decade 4

Our Father...

They divide my clothes among themselves, and for my clothing they cast lots. (Ps 22:18, NRSVCE)
Hail Mary...

Into your hand I commit my spirit; you have redeemed me, O Lord, faithful God. (Ps 31:5, NRSVCE)
Hail Mary...

All my enemies, and especially my neighbors, treat me with contempt. Those who know me are afraid of me; when they see me in the street, they run away. (Ps 31:11, GNT)
Hail Mary...

I hear the whispering of many — terror all around! — as they scheme together against me, as they plot to take my life. (Ps 31:13, NRSVCE)
Hail Mary...

Insults have broken my heart, and I am in despair. I had hoped for sympathy, but there was none; for comfort, but I found none. When I was hungry, they gave me poison; when I was thirsty, they offered me vinegar. (Ps 69:20-21, GNT)
Hail Mary...

I shall not die, but I shall live, and recount the deeds of the Lord. (Ps 118:17, NRSVCE)
Hail Mary...

I will place the key of the house of David upon his shoulder. And when he opens, no one will close. And when he closes, no one will open. And I will fasten him like a peg in a trustworthy place. And he will be upon a throne of glory in the house of his father. (Is 22:22-23)
Hail Mary...

He said to them: "How foolish and reluctant in heart you are, to believe everything that has been spoken by the Prophets! Was not the Christ required to suffer these things, and so enter into his glory?" And beginning from Moses and all the Prophets, he interpreted for them, in all the Scriptures, the things that were about him. (Luk 24:25-27)
Hail Mary...

I will strike a covenant of peace with them. This will be an everlasting covenant for them. And I will establish them, and multiply them. And I will set my sanctuary in their midst, unceasingly. And my tabernacle shall be among them. And I will be their God, and they will be my people. (Eze 37:26-27)
Hail Mary...

I will allot to him a great number. And he will divide the spoils of the strong. For he has handed over his life to death, and he was reputed among criminals. And he has taken away the sins of many, and he has prayed for the transgressors. (Is 53:12)
Hail Mary...

Glory Be...

Decade 5

Our Father...

Behold, I will set a stone within the foundations of Zion, a tested stone, a cornerstone, a precious stone, which has been established in the foundation: whoever trusts in him need not hurry. (Is 28:16)
Hail Mary...

I have given my body to those who strike me, and my cheeks to those who plucked them. I have not averted my face from those who rebuked me and who spit on me. (Is 50:6)
Hail Mary...

Behold, my servant will understand; he will be exalted and lifted up, and he will be very sublime. (Is 52:13)
Hail Mary...

Many people were shocked when they saw him; he was so disfigured that he hardly looked human. (Is 52:14, GNT)
Hail Mary...

Many nations will marvel at him, and kings will be speechless with amazement. They will see and understand something they had never known. (Is 52:15, NRSVCE)
Hail Mary...

He was lifted up from anguish and judgment. Who will describe his life? For he has been cut off from the land of the living. Because of the wickedness of my people, I have struck him down. (Is 53:8)
Hail Mary...

He will be given a place with the impious for his burial, and with the rich for his death, though he has done no iniquity, nor was deceit in his mouth. (Is 53:9)
Hail Mary...

It was the will of the Lord to crush him with infirmity. If he lays down his life because of sin, he will see offspring with long lives, and the will of the Lord will be directed by his hand. (Is 53:10)
Hail Mary...

His reign will be increased, and there will be no end to his peace. He will sit upon the throne of David and over his kingdom, to confirm and strengthen it, in judgment and justice, from now even unto eternity. The zeal of the Lord of hosts shall accomplish this. (Is 9:7)
Hail Mary...

I shall see him, but not presently. I shall gaze upon him, but not soon. A star shall rise out of Jacob, and a rod shall spring up from Israel. (Num 24:17)
Hail Mary...

Glory Be...

Who is Jesus?

Decade 1

Our Father…

In the past God spoke to our ancestors many times and in many ways through the prophets, but in these last days he has spoken to us through his Son. He is the one through whom God created the universe, the one whom God has chosen to possess all things at the end. (Heb 1:1-2, GNT)
Hail Mary…

He reflects the brightness of God's glory and is the exact likeness of God's own being, sustaining the universe with his powerful word. After achieving forgiveness for the sins of all human beings, he sat down in heaven at the right side of God, the Supreme Power. (Heb 1:3, GNT)
Hail Mary…

This man, offering one sacrifice for sins, sits at the right hand of God forever, awaiting that time when his enemies will be made his footstool. (Heb 10:12-13)
Hail Mary…

You know the grace of our Lord Jesus Christ, that though he was rich, he became poor for your sakes, so that through his poverty, you might become rich. (2 Cor 8:9)
Hail Mary…

Though he was in the form of God, did not consider equality with God something to be seized. Instead, he emptied himself, taking the form of a servant, being made in the likeness of men, and accepting the state of a man. He humbled himself, becoming obedient even unto death, even the death of the Cross. (Phil 2:6-8)
Hail Mary…

God has also exalted him and has given him a name which is above every name, so that, at the name of Jesus, every knee would bend, of those in heaven, of those on earth, and of those in hell, and so that every tongue would confess that the Lord Jesus Christ is in the glory of God the Father. (Phil 2:9-11)

Hail Mary…

Christ, having been offered once to bear the sins of many, will appear a second time, not to deal with sin, but to save those who are eagerly waiting for him. (Heb 9:28, NRSVCE)
Hail Mary…

When the right time finally came, God sent his own Son. He came as the son of a human mother and lived under the Jewish Law, to redeem those who were under the Law, so that we might become God's children. (Gal 4:4-5, GNT)
Hail Mary…

He is the image of the invisible God, the first-born of every creature. For in him was created everything in heaven and on earth, visible and invisible, whether thrones, or dominations, or principalities, or powers. All things were created through him and in him. (Col 1:15-16)
Hail Mary…

Christ existed before all things, and in union with him all things have their proper place. He is the head of his body, the church; he is the source of the body's life. He is the first-born Son, who was raised from death, in order that he alone might have the first place in all things. (Col 1:17-18)
Hail Mary…

Glory Be…

Decade 2

Our Father…

In him all the fullness of God was pleased to dwell, and through him God was pleased to reconcile to himself all things, whether on earth or in heaven, by making peace through the blood of his cross. (Col 1:19-20, NRSVCE)
Hail Mary…

Christ has redeemed us from the curse of the law, since he became a curse for us. For it is written: "Cursed is anyone who hangs from a tree." (Gal 3:13)
Hail Mary…

Christ was without sin, but for our sake God made him share our sin in order that in union with him we might share the righteousness of God. (2 Cor 5:21, GNT)
Hail Mary…

All of you, my fellow Israelites, are to know for sure that it is through Jesus that the message about forgiveness of sins is preached to you; you are to know that everyone who believes in him is set free from all the sins from which the Law of Moses could not set you free. (Acts 13:38-39, GNT)
Hail Mary…

You know that it was not with corruptible gold or silver that you were redeemed away from your useless behavior in the traditions of your fathers, but it was with the precious blood of Christ, an immaculate and undefiled lamb. (1 Pet 1:18-19)
Hail Mary…

He had been chosen by God before the creation of the world and was revealed in these last days for your sake. Through him you believe in God, who raised him from death and gave him glory; and so your faith and hope are fixed on God. (1 Pet 1:20-21, GNT)
Hail Mary…

We understand that Jesus, who was reduced to a little less than the Angels, was crowned with glory and honor because of his passion and death, in order that, by the grace of God, he might taste death for all. (Heb 2:9)
Hail Mary…

Since the children, as he calls them, are people of flesh and blood, Jesus himself became like them and shared their human nature. He did this so that through his death he might destroy the Devil, who has the power over death, and in this way set free those who were slaves all their lives because of their fear of death. (Heb 2:14-15, GNT)
Hail Mary…

He had to become like his people in every way, in order to be their faithful and merciful High Priest in his service to God, so that the people's sins would be forgiven. (Heb 2:17, GNT)
Hail Mary…

We do not have a high priest who is unable to have compassion on our infirmities, but rather one who was tempted in all things, just as we are, yet without sin. (Heb 4:15)
Hail Mary…

Glory Be…

Decade 3

Our Father…

It is Christ who, in the days of his flesh, with a strong cry and tears, offered prayers and supplications to the One who was able to save him from death, and who was heard because of his reverence. (Heb 5:7)
Hail Mary…

Even though he was God's Son, he learned through his sufferings to be obedient. When he was made perfect, he became the source of eternal salvation for all those who obey him, and God declared him to be high priest, in the priestly order of Melchizedek. (Heb 5:8-10, GNT)
Hail Mary…

Come to the Lord, the living stone rejected by people as worthless but chosen by God as valuable. (1 Pet 2:4, GNT)
Hail Mary…

Christ also died once for our sins, the Just One on behalf of the unjust, so that he might offer us to God, having died, certainly, in the flesh, but having been enlivened by the Spirit. (1 Pet 3:18)
Hail Mary…

Jesus did not enter by means of holy things made with hands, mere examples of the true things, but he entered into Heaven itself, so that he may appear now before the face of God for us. (Heb 9:24)
Hail Mary…

While we were still weak, at the right time Christ died for the ungodly. Indeed, rarely will anyone die for a righteous person — though perhaps for a good person someone might actually dare to die. (Rom 5:6-7, NRSVCE)
Hail Mary…

We were God's enemies, but he made us his friends through the death of his Son. Now that we are God's friends, how much more will we be saved by Christ's life! (Rom 5:10, GNT)
Hail Mary...

We know that Christ, in rising up from the dead, can no longer die: death no longer has dominion over him. For in as much as he died for sin, he died once. But in as much as he lives, he lives for God. (Rom 6:9-10)
Hail Mary...

There is one God, and one mediator of God and of men, the man Christ Jesus, who gave himself as a redemption for all, as a testimony in its proper time. (1 Tim 2:5-6)
Hail Mary...

Jesus is the one of whom the scripture says, 'The stone that you the builders despised turned out to be the most important of all.' Salvation is to be found through him alone; in all the world there is no one else whom God has given who can save us. (Acts 4:11-12, GNT)
Hail Mary...

Glory Be...

Decade 4

Our Father...

These shall fight against the Lamb, and the Lamb shall conquer them. For he is the Lord of lords and the King of kings. And those who are with him are called, and chosen, and faithful. (Rev 17:14)
Hail Mary...

For if you confess with your mouth the Lord Jesus, and if you believe in your heart that God has raised him up from the dead, you shall be saved. (Rom 10:9)
Hail Mary...

I am the Alpha and the Omega, the First and the Last, the Beginning and the End. (Rev 22:13)
Hail Mary...

Let us run with perseverance the race that is set before us, looking to Jesus the pioneer and perfecter of our faith, who for the sake of the

joy that was set before him endured the cross, disregarding its shame, and has taken his seat at the right hand of the throne of God. (Heb 12:1-2, NRSVCE)
Hail Mary...

He is the propitiation for our sins. And not only for our sins, but also for those of the whole world. (1 Jn 2:2)
Hail Mary...

This man, because he continues forever, has an everlasting priesthood. And for this reason, he is able, continuously, to save those who approach God through him, since he is ever alive to make intercession on our behalf. (Heb 7:24-25)
Hail Mary...

God did not send his Son into the world, in order to judge the world, but in order that the world may be saved through him. (Jn 3:17)
Hail Mary...

Jesus Christ is the same yesterday, today, and forever. (Heb 13:8)
Hail Mary...

We know that the Son of God has arrived, and that he has given us understanding, so that we may know the true God, and so that we may remain in his true Son. This is the true God, and this is Eternal Life. (1 Jn 5:20)
Hail Mary...

He has been granted a better ministry, so much so that he is also the Mediator of a better testament, which has been confirmed by better promises. (Heb 8:6)
Hail Mary...

Glory Be...

Decade 5

Our Father...

He was with God in the beginning. (Jn 1:2)
Hail Mary...

All things were made through Him, and nothing that was made was made without Him. (Jn 1:3)
Hail Mary...

What has come into being in him was life, and the life was the light of all people. (Jn 1:3-4, NRSVCE)
Hail Mary…

He was in the world, and the world was made through him, and the world did not recognize him. (Jn 1:10)
Hail Mary…

He went to his own, and his own did not accept him. (Jn 1:11)
Hail Mary…

Yet whoever did accept him, those who believed in his name, he gave them the power to become the sons of God. These are born, not of blood, nor of the will of flesh, nor of the will of man, but of God. (Jn 1:12-13)
Hail Mary…

And the Word became flesh, and he lived among us, and we saw his glory, glory like that of an only-begotten Son from the Father, full of grace and truth. (Jn 1:14)
Hail Mary…

John spoke about him. He cried out, "This is the one I was talking about when I said, 'He comes after me, but he is greater than I am, because he existed before I was born.'" Out of the fullness of his grace he has blessed us all, giving us one blessing after another. (Jn 1:15-16, GNT)
Hail Mary…

The law was given through Moses, but grace and truth came through Jesus Christ. (Jn 1:17)
Hail Mary…

No one has ever seen God. The only Son, who is the same as God and is at the Father's side, he has made him known. (Jn 1:18, NRSVCE)
Hail Mary…

Glory Be…

Words of Jesus

Decade 1

Our Father…

You are the salt of the earth. But if salt loses its saltiness, with what will it be salted? It is no longer useful at all, except to be cast out and trampled under by men. (Matt 5:13)
Hail Mary…

No one lights a lamp and puts it under a bowl; instead it is put on the lampstand, where it gives light for everyone in the house. In the same way your light must shine before people, so that they will see the good things you do and praise your Father in heaven. (Matt 5:15-16, GNT)
Hail Mary…

Watch out! Don't do your good deeds publicly, to be admired by others, for you will lose the reward from your Father in heaven. (Matt 6:1, NLT)
Hail Mary…

Do not be worried about the food and drink you need in order to stay alive, or about clothes for your body. After all, isn't life worth more than food? And isn't the body worth more than clothes? (Matt 6:25, GNT)
Hail Mary…

Seek first the kingdom of God and his justice, and all these things shall be added to you as well. (Matt 6:33)
Hail Mary…

Go in through the narrow gate, because the gate to hell is wide and the road that leads to it is easy, and there are many who travel it. But the gate to life is narrow and the way that leads to it is hard, and there are few people who find it. (Matt 7:13-14, GNT)
Hail Mary…

Do not be afraid of those who kill the body, but are not able to kill the soul. But instead fear him who is able to destroy both soul and body in Hell. (Matt 10:28)

43

Hail Mary...

All things have been delivered to me by my Father. And no one knows the Son except the Father, nor does anyone know the Father except the Son, and those to whom the Son is willing to reveal him. (Matt 11:27)
Hail Mary...

Come to me, all you that are weary and are carrying heavy burdens, and I will give you rest. (Matt 11:28, NRSVCE)
Hail Mary...

If anyone is willing to come after me, let him deny himself, and take up his cross, and follow me. (Matt 16:24)
Hail Mary...Glory Be…

Decade 2

Our Father…

The greatest among you will be your servant. (Matt 23:11, NRSVCE)
Hail Mary...

Whoever has exalted himself, shall be humbled. And whoever has humbled himself, shall be exalted. (Matt 23:12)
Hail Mary...

For whoever has done the will of God, the same is my brother, and my sister and mother. (Mrk 3:35)
Hail Mary...

Those who have something will be given more, and those who have nothing will have taken away from them even the little they have. (Mrk 4:25, GNT)
Hail Mary...

Go to your own people, in your own house, and announce to them how great are the things that the Lord has done for you, and how he has taken pity on you. (Mrk 5:19)
Hail Mary...

Whoever will have chosen to save his life, will lose it. But whoever will have lost his life, for my sake and for the Gospel, shall save it. (Mrk 8:35)
Hail Mary...

What shall it profit a man, if he gain the whole world, and suffer the loss of his soul? Or what shall a man give in exchange for his soul? (Mrk 8:36-37, DRA)
Hail Mary...

Allow the little ones to come to me, and do not prohibit them. For of such as these is the kingdom of God. Amen I say to you, whoever will not accept the kingdom of God like a little child, will not enter into it. (Mrk 10:14-15)
Hail Mary...

It is easier for a camel to pass through the eye of a needle, than for the rich to enter into the kingdom of God. (Mrk 10:25)
Hail Mary...

Amen I say to you, There is no one who has left behind house, or brothers, or sisters, or father, or mother, or children, or land, for my sake and for the Gospel, who will not receive one hundred times as much, now in this time: houses, and brothers, and sisters, and mothers, and children, and land, with persecutions, and in the future age eternal life. (Mrk 10:29-30)
Hail Mary...Glory Be...

Decade 3

Our Father...

Whoever wishes to become great among you must be your servant, and whoever wishes to be first among you must be slave of all. For the Son of Man came not to be served but to serve, and to give his life a ransom for many. (Mrk 10:43-45, NRSVCE)
Hail Mary...

Watch and pray, so that you may not enter into temptation. The spirit indeed is willing, but the flesh is weak. (Mrk 14:38, NRSVCE)
Hail Mary...

To him who strikes you on the cheek, offer the other also. And from him who takes away your coat, do not withhold even your tunic. (Luk 6:29)
Hail Mary...

Whoever will be ashamed of me and of my words: of him the Son of man will be ashamed, when he will have arrived in his majesty and that of his Father and of the holy Angels. (Luk 9:26)
Hail Mary...

Certainly the harvest is great, but the workers are few. Therefore, ask the Lord of the harvest to send workers into his harvest. (Luk 10:2)
Hail Mary...

Whoever listens to you listens to me; whoever rejects you rejects me; and whoever rejects me rejects the one who sent me. (Luk 10:16, GNT)
Hail Mary...

Father, Lord of heaven and earth! I thank you because you have shown to the unlearned what you have hidden from the wise and learned. Yes, Father, this was how you were pleased to have it happen. (Luk 10:21, GNT)
Hail Mary...

Whoever is not with me is against me, and whoever does not gather with me scatters. (Luk 11:23, NRSVCE)
Hail Mary...

Do not be fearful of those who kill the body, and afterwards have no more that they can do. But I will reveal to you whom you should fear. Fear him who, after he will have killed, has the power to cast into Hell. So I say to you: Fear him. (Luk 12:4-5)
Hail Mary...

Watch out and guard yourselves from every kind of greed; because your true life is not made up of the things you own, no matter how rich you may be. (Luk 12:15, GNT)
Hail Mary...Glory Be...

Decade 4

Our Father...

Strive to enter through the narrow gate. For many, I tell you, will seek to enter and not be able. (Luk 13:24)
Hail Mary...

For everyone who exalts himself shall be humbled, and whoever humbles himself shall be exalted. (Luk 14:11)

Hail Mary...

If anyone comes to me, and does not hate his father, and mother, and wife, and children, and brothers, and sisters, and yes, even his own life, he is not able to be my disciple. (Luk 14:26)
Hail Mary...

Whoever is faithful in small matters will be faithful in large ones; whoever is dishonest in small matters will be dishonest in large ones. (Luk 16:10, GNT)
Hail Mary...

If you knew the gift of God, and who it is who is saying to you, 'Give me to drink,' perhaps you would have made a request of him, and he would have given you living water. (Jn 4:10)
Hail Mary...

God is Spirit. And so, those who worship him must worship in spirit and in truth. (Jn 4:24)
Hail Mary...

I tell you the truth: the Son can do nothing on his own; he does only what he sees his Father doing. What the Father does, the Son also does. (Jn 5:19, GNT)
Hail Mary...

No one is able to come to me, unless the Father, who has sent me, has drawn him. And I will raise him up on the last day. (Jn 6:44)
Hail Mary...

It is the spirit that gives life; the flesh is useless. The words that I have spoken to you are spirit and life. (Jn 6:63, NRSVCE)
Hail Mary...

I am the light of the world. Whoever follows me does not walk in darkness, but shall have the light of life. (Jn 8:12)
Hail Mary...Glory Be...

Decade 5

Our Father...

He who sent me is with me, and he has not abandoned me alone. For I always do what is pleasing to him. (Jn 8:29)
Hail Mary...

47

I am the gate. Those who come in through me will be saved. They will come and go freely and will find good pastures. (Jn 10:9, NLT)
Hail Mary...

The thief comes only in order to steal, kill, and destroy. I have come in order that you might have life — life in all its fullness. (Jn 10:10, GNT)
Hail Mary...

I am the good Shepherd. The good Shepherd gives his life for his sheep. (Jn 10:11)
Hail Mary...

The Father loves me because I sacrifice my life so I may take it back again. No one can take my life from me. I sacrifice it voluntarily. For I have the authority to lay it down when I want to and also to take it up again. For this is what my Father has commanded. (Jn 10:17-18, NLT)
Hail Mary...

I am the Resurrection and the Life. Whoever believes in me, even though he has died, he shall live. (Jn 11:25)
Hail Mary...

I am the Way, and the Truth, and the Life. No one comes to the Father, except through me. (Jn 14:6)
Hail Mary...

I am the vine; you are the branches. Whoever abides in me, and I in him, bears much fruit. For without me, you are able to do nothing. (Jn 15:5)
Hail Mary...

Do not let your heart be troubled. You believe in God. Believe in me also. (Jn 14:1)
Hail Mary...

All who love me will do what I say. My Father will love them, and we will come and make our home with each of them. (Jn 14:23, NLT)
Hail Mary...Glory Be...

The Word of God

Decade 1

Our Father...

One does not live by bread alone, but by every word that comes from the mouth of God. (Matt 4:4, NRSVCE)
Hail Mary...

Is not my word like fire, says the Lord, and like a hammer that breaks a rock in pieces? (Jer 23:29)
Hail Mary...

The Word of God is living and effective: more piercing than any two-edged sword, reaching to the division even between the soul and the spirit, even between the joints and the marrow, and so it discerns the thoughts and intentions of the heart. (Heb 4:12)
Hail Mary...

Your word is a lamp to my feet and a light to my path. (Ps 119:105, NRSVCE)
Hail Mary...

Neither herb, nor poultice, healed them, but your word, O Lord, which heals all. (Wis 16:12)
Hail Mary...

If you will abide in my word, you will truly be my disciples. And you shall know the truth, and the truth shall set you free. (Jn 8:31-32)
Hail Mary...

Happy are those who reject the advice of evil people, who do not follow the example of sinners or join those who have no use for God. Instead, they find joy in obeying the Law of the Lord, and they study it day and night. (Ps 1:1-2, GNT)
Hail Mary...

In the beginning was the Word, and the Word was with God, and God was the Word. (Jn 1:1)
Hail Mary...

Blessed is he who reads or hears the words of this Prophecy, and who keeps the things that have been written in it. (Rev 1:3)
Hail Mary...

All Scripture, having been divinely inspired, is useful for teaching, for reproof, for correction, and for instruction in justice, so that the man of God may be perfect, having been trained for every good work. (2 Tim 3:16-17)
Hail Mary...

Glory Be...

Decade 2

Our Father...

Amen, amen, I say to you, that whoever hears my word, and believes in him who sent me, has eternal life, and he does not go into judgment, but instead he crosses from death into life. (Jn 5:24)
Hail Mary...

How can young people keep their way pure? By guarding it according to your word. (Ps 119:9, NRSVCE)
Hail Mary...

I treasure your word in my heart, so that I may not sin against you. (Ps 119:11, NRSVCE)
Hail Mary...

Great peace have those who love your law; nothing can make them stumble. (Ps 119:165, NRSVCE)
Hail Mary...

Give attention to the public reading of scripture, to exhorting, to teaching. (1 Tim 4:13, NRSVCE)
Hail Mary...

I discovered your words and I consumed them. And your word became to me as the gladness and joy of my heart. For your name has been invoked over me, O Lord, the God of hosts. (Jer 15:16)
Hail Mary...

As the rain and the snow come down from heaven, and do not return there until they have watered the earth, making it bring forth and

sprout, giving seed to the sower and bread to the eater, so shall my word be that goes out from my mouth; it shall not return to me empty, but it shall accomplish that which I purpose, and succeed in the thing for which I sent it. (Is 55:10-11, NRSVCE)
Hail Mary...

The law of the Lord is perfect; it gives new strength. The commands of the Lord are trustworthy, giving wisdom to those who lack it. The laws of the Lord are right, and those who obey them are happy. The commands of the Lord are just and give understanding to the mind. (Ps 19:7-8, GNT)
Hail Mary...

My child, pay attention to what I say. Listen to my words. Never let them get away from you. Remember them and keep them in your heart. They will give life and health to anyone who understands them. (Pro 4:20-22, GNT)
Hail Mary...

Whatever was written, was written to teach us, so that, through patience and the consolation of the Scriptures, we might have hope. (Rom 15:4)
Hail Mary...

Glory Be...

Decade 3

Our Father...

Faith comes from what is heard, and what is heard comes through the word of Christ. (Rom 10:17)
Hail Mary...

Heaven and earth shall pass away, but my words shall not pass away. (Matt 24:35)
Hail Mary...

The book of this law shall not depart from your mouth. Instead, you shall meditate upon it, day and night, so that you may observe and do all the things that are written in it. Then you shall direct your way and understand it. (Josh 1:8)
Hail Mary...

For this reason, it is necessary for us to observe more thoroughly the things that we have heard, lest we let them slip away. (Heb 2:1)
Hail Mary...

Get rid of every filthy habit and all wicked conduct. Submit to God and accept the word that he plants in your hearts, which is able to save you. (Jas 1:21, GNT)
Hail Mary...

The mouths of the righteous utter wisdom, and their tongues speak justice. The law of their God is in their hearts; their steps do not slip. (Ps 37:30-31, NRSVCE)
Hail Mary...

I am not ashamed of the Gospel. For it is the power of God unto salvation for all believers, the Jew first, and the Greek. (Rom 1:16)
Hail Mary...

He who gazes upon the perfect law of liberty, and who remains in it, is not a forgetful hearer, but instead a doer of the work. He shall be blessed in what he does. (Jas 1:25)
Hail Mary...

The grass has dried up, and the flower has fallen. But the Word of our Lord remains for eternity. (Is 40:8)
Hail Mary...

First of all you must understand this, that no prophecy of scripture is a matter of one's own interpretation, because no prophecy ever came by human will, but men and women moved by the Holy Spirit spoke from God. (2 Pet 1:20-21, NRSVCE)
Hail Mary...

Glory Be...

Decade 4

Our Father...

Everyone who hears these words of mine and does them shall be compared to a wise man, who built his house upon the rock. And the rains descended, and the floods rose up, and the winds blew, and rushed upon that house, but it did not fall, for it was founded on the rock. (Matt 7:24-25)

Hail Mary...

The Lord created the heavens by his command, the sun, moon, and stars by his spoken word. (Ps 33:6, GNT)
Hail Mary...

I will never neglect your instructions, because by them you have kept me alive. (Ps 119:93, GNT)
Hail Mary...

The promises of the Lord can be trusted; they are as genuine as silver refined seven times in the furnace. (Ps 12:6, GNT)
Hail Mary...

Until heaven and earth pass away, not one letter, not one stroke of a letter, will pass from the law until all is accomplished. (Matt 5:18, NRSVCE)
Hail Mary...

The word of the Lord is upright, and all his work is done in faithfulness. (Ps 33:4, NRSVCE)
Hail Mary...

Be doers of the Word, and not listeners only, deceiving yourselves. (Jas 1:22)
Hail Mary...

Give ear, O my people, to my teaching; incline your ears to the words of my mouth. (Ps 78:1, NRSVCE)
Hail Mary...

Make my teaching your treasure and joy, and you will be well instructed. (Wis 6:11, GNT)
Hail Mary...

Never forget these commands that I am giving you today. Teach them to your children. Repeat them when you are at home and when you are away, when you are resting and when you are working. Tie them on your arms and wear them on your foreheads as a reminder. Write them on the doorposts of your houses and on your gates. (Deut 6:6-9, GNT)
Hail Mary...

Glory Be...

Decade 5

Our Father…

If your law had not been the source of my joy, I would have died from my sufferings. (Ps 119:92, GNT)
Hail Mary…

Devote all your time to studying the Lord's commands and thinking about them. He will give you the insight and wisdom you are looking for. (Sir 6:37, GNT)
Hail Mary…

You have been born again, not from corruptible seed, but from what is incorruptible, from the Word of God, living and remaining for all eternity. (1 Pet 1:23)
Hail Mary…

All flesh is like the grass and all its glory is like the flower of the grass. The grass withers and its flower falls away. But the Word of the Lord endures for eternity. (1 Pet 1:24)
Hail Mary…

Let the word of Christ live in you in abundance, with all wisdom, teaching and correcting one another, with Psalms, hymns, and spiritual canticles, singing to God with the grace in your hearts. (Col 3:16)
Hail Mary…

Anyone who does not stay with the teaching of Christ, but goes beyond it, does not have God. Whoever does stay with the teaching has both the Father and the Son. (2 Jn 1:9, GNT)
Hail Mary…

The unfolding of your words gives light; it imparts understanding to the simple. (Ps 119:130, NRSVCE)
Hail Mary…

I delight in following your commands more than in having great wealth. I study your instructions; I examine your teachings. I take pleasure in your laws; your commands I will not forget. (Ps 119:14-16, GNT)
Hail Mary…

This is my comfort in my distress, that your promise gives me life. (Ps 119:50, NRSVCE)
Hail Mary...

This God — his way is perfect; the promise of the Lord proves true; he is a shield for all who take refuge in him. (Ps 18:30, NRSVCE)
Hail Mary..

Glory Be…

Spiritual Warfare & Deliverance Scriptures

Decade 1

Our Father…

And now I will break off his yoke from you and snap the bonds that bind you. (Nah 1:13, NRSVCE)
Hail Mary…

The Lord has redeemed Jacob, and he has freed him from the hand of one more powerful. (Jer 31:11)
Hail Mary…

He sent out his word and healed them, and delivered them from destruction. (Ps 107:20, NRSVCE)
Hail Mary…

They cried to the Lord in their trouble, and he saved them from their distress; he brought them out of darkness and gloom, and broke their bonds asunder. (Ps 107:13-14, NRSVCE)
Hail Mary…

Behold, I have given you authority to tread upon serpents and scorpions, and upon all the powers of the enemy, and nothing shall hurt you. (Luk 10:19)
Hail Mary…

May the God of peace quickly crush Satan under your feet. The grace of our Lord Jesus Christ be with you. (Rom 16:20)
Hail Mary…

If the righteous man is God's child, he will help him, and will deliver him from the hand of his adversaries. (Wis 2:18, NRSVCE)
Hail Mary…

Whenever the evil spirit from the Lord assailed Saul, David took up his stringed instrument, and he struck it with his hand, and Saul was refreshed and uplifted. For the evil spirit withdrew from him. (1 Sam 16:23)
Hail Mary…

Let my supplication come before you; deliver me according to your promise. (Ps 119:170, NRSVCE)
Hail Mary...

When that day comes, I will break the yoke that is around their neck and remove their chains, and they will no longer be the slaves of foreigners. Instead, they will serve me, the Lord their God. (Jer 30:8-9, GNT)
Hail Mary...

Glory Be...

Decade 2

Our Father...

Take courage, my children, and cry out to God for help. He will rescue you from oppression, from the power of your enemies. (Bar 4:21, GNT)
Hail Mary...

The Lord will cause your enemies who rise against you to be defeated before you; they shall come out against you one way, and flee before you seven ways. (Deut 28:7, NRSVCE)
Hail Mary...

No weapon that is fashioned against you shall prosper, and you shall confute every tongue that rises against you in judgment. (Is 54:17, NRSVCE)
Hail Mary...

For though we walk in the flesh, we do not battle according to the flesh. (2 Cor 10:3)
Hail Mary...

Be strong in the Lord and in the strength of his power. Put on the whole armor of God, so that you may be able to stand against the wiles of the devil. For our struggle is not against enemies of blood and flesh, but against the rulers, against the authorities, against the cosmic powers of this present darkness, against the spiritual forces of evil in the heavenly places. (Eph 6:10-12, NRSVCE)
Hail Mary...

Therefore take up the whole armor of God, so that you may be able to withstand on that evil day, and having done everything, to stand firm. Stand therefore, and fasten the belt of truth around your waist, and put on the breastplate of righteousness. As shoes for your feet put on whatever will make you ready to proclaim the gospel of peace. With all of these, take the shield of faith, with which you will be able to quench all the flaming arrows of the evil one. Take the helmet of salvation, and the sword of the Spirit, which is the word of God. (Eph 6:13-17, NRSVCE)
Hail Mary...

He has rescued us from the power of darkness, and he has transferred us into the kingdom of the Son of his love. (Col 1:13)
Hail Mary...

God is faithful. He will strengthen you, and he will guard you from evil. (2 Thes 3:3)
Hail Mary...

I struck them down, so that they were not able to rise; they fell under my feet. For you girded me with strength for the battle; you made my assailants sink under me. (Ps 18:38-39, NRSVCE)
Hail Mary...

Through you we push down our foes; through your name we tread down our assailants. (Ps 44:5, NRSVCE)
Hail Mary...

Glory Be...

Decade 3

Our Father...

The Lord is a stronghold for the oppressed, a stronghold in times of trouble. (Ps 9:9, NRSVCE)
Hail Mary...

He delivered me, because he delighted in me. (Ps 18:19, NRSVCE)
Hail Mary...

Though an army encamp against me, my heart shall not fear; though war rise up against me, yet I will be confident. (Ps 27:3, NRSVCE)
Hail Mary...

Let God rise up, let his enemies be scattered; let those who hate him flee before him. As smoke is driven away, so drive them away; as wax melts before the fire, let the wicked perish before God. (Ps 68:1-2, NRSVCE)
Hail Mary...

A thousand may fall at your side, ten thousand at your right hand, but it will not come near you. You will only look with your eyes and see the punishment of the wicked. (Ps 91:7-8, NRSVCE)
Hail Mary...

Little children, you are from God, and have conquered them; for the one who is in you is greater than the one who is in the world. (1 Jn 4:4, NRSVCE)
Hail Mary...

If God is for us, who is against us? (Rom 8:31)
Hail Mary...

Now these signs will accompany those who believe. In my name, they shall cast out demons. They will speak in new languages. They will take up serpents, and, if they drink anything deadly, it will not harm them. They shall lay their hands upon the sick, and they will be well. (Mrk 16:17-18)
Hail Mary...

Submit yourselves to God. Resist the Devil, and he will run away from you. Come near to God, and he will come near to you. (Jas 4:7-8, GNT)
Hail Mary...

You should not fear them. For the Lord your God will fight on your behalf. (Deut 3:22)
Hail Mary...

Glory Be...

Decade 4

Our Father...

Your hand shall be lifted up over your adversaries, and all your enemies shall be cut off. (Mic 5:9, NRSVCE)
Hail Mary...

Rise up, O Lord, and let your enemies be scattered, and let those who hate you flee from your face. (Num 10:35)
Hail Mary...

You, my enemy, should not rejoice over me because I have fallen. I will rise up, when I sit in darkness. The Lord is my light. (Mic 7:8)
Hail Mary...

One of you shall pursue a thousand men of the enemies. For the Lord your God himself will fight on your behalf, just as he promised. (Josh 23:10)
Hail Mary...

Jesus called the twelve disciples together and gave them power and authority to drive out all demons and to cure diseases. (Luk 9:1, GNT)
Hail Mary...

Amen I say to you, whatever you will have bound on earth, shall be bound also in heaven, and whatever you will have released on earth, shall be released also in heaven. (Matt 18:18)
Hail Mary...

The weapons we use in our fight are not the world's weapons but God's powerful weapons, which we use to destroy strongholds. We destroy false arguments; we pull down every proud obstacle that is raised against the knowledge of God; we take every thought captive and make it obey Christ. (2 Cor 10:4-5, GNT)
Hail Mary...

When evening came, people brought to Jesus many who had demons in them. Jesus drove out the evil spirits with a word and healed all who were sick. (Matt 8:16, GNT)
Hail Mary...

The Lord God himself, who is your leader, will fight on your behalf, just as he did in Egypt in the sight of all. (Deut 1:30)
Hail Mary...

The souls of the just are in the hand of God and no torment of death will touch them. (Wis 3:1)
Hail Mary...

Glory Be...

Decade 5

Our Father…

If the righteous really are God's children, God will save them from their enemies. (Wis 2:18, GNT)
Hail Mary…

Do not be afraid. Neither should you be dismayed by this multitude. For the fight is not yours, but God's. (2 Chron 20:15)
Hail Mary…

The Lord has freed me from every evil work, and he will accomplish salvation by his heavenly kingdom. To him be glory forever and ever. Amen. (2 Tim 4:18)
Hail Mary…

I call upon the Lord, who is worthy to be praised, so I shall be saved from my enemies. (Ps 18:3, NRSVCE)
Hail Mary…

Be sober and vigilant. For your adversary, the devil, is like a roaring lion, traveling around and seeking those whom he might devour. Resist him by being strong in faith. (1 Pet 5:8-9)
Hail Mary…

All who are incensed against you shall be ashamed and disgraced; those who strive against you shall be as nothing and shall perish. You shall seek those who contend with you, but you shall not find them; those who war against you shall be as nothing at all. For I, the Lord your God, hold your right hand; it is I who say to you, "Do not fear, I will help you. (Is 41:11-13, NRSVCE)
Hail Mary…

I will present you to this people as a strong wall of brass. And they will fight against you, and they will not prevail. For I am with you, so as to save you and to rescue you, says the Lord. (Jer 15:20)
Hail Mary…

Do not be afraid. Stand firm and see the great wonders of the Lord, which he will do today. For the Egyptians, whom you now see, will never again be seen, forever. The Lord will fight on your behalf, and you will remain silent. (Exo 14:13-14)
Hail Mary…

On the day when I act, you will overcome the wicked, and they will be like dust under your feet. (Mal 4:3, GNT)
Hail Mary...

Because you have made the Lord your refuge, the Most High your dwelling place, no evil shall befall you, no scourge come near your tent. (Ps 91:9, NRSVCE)
Hail Mary..

Glory Be...

Healing Scriptures

Decade 1

Our Father...

If you will listen to the voice of the Lord your God, and do what is right in his sight, and obey his commands, and keep all his precepts, I will not bring upon you any of the distress that I imposed on Egypt. For I am the Lord, your healer. (Exo 15:26)
Hail Mary...

O Lord my God, I cried to you for help, and you have healed me. (Ps 30:2, NRSVCE)
Hail Mary...

Bless the Lord, O my soul, and do not forget all his benefits—who forgives all your iniquity, who heals all your diseases. (Ps 103:2-3, NRSVCE)
Hail Mary...

Heal me, O Lord, and I will be healed. Save me, and I will be saved. For you are my praise. (Jer 17:14)
Hail Mary...

You shall serve the Lord your God, so that I may bless your bread and your waters, and so that I may take away sickness from your midst. There will not be fruitless or barren ones in your land. I will fill up the number of your days. (Exo 23:25-26)
Hail Mary...

When the sun had set, all those who had anyone afflicted with various diseases brought them to him. Then, laying his hands on each one of them, he cured them. (Luk 4:40)
Hail Mary...

Many crowds followed him, and he cured all of them. (Matt 12:15)
Hail Mary

The entire city was gathered together at the door. And he healed many who were troubled with various illnesses. And he cast out many demons. (Mrk 1:33-34)

Hail Mary...

The blind and the lame drew near to him in the temple; and he healed them. (Matt 21:14)
Hail Mary...

The people recognized Jesus. So they sent for the sick people in all the surrounding country and brought them to Jesus. They begged him to let the sick at least touch the edge of his cloak; and all who touched it were made well. (Matt 14:35-36, GNT)
Hail Mary...

Glory Be…

Decade 2

Our Father…

Great multitudes came to him, having with them the mute, the blind, the lame, the disabled, and many others. And they cast them down at his feet, and he cured them. (Matt 15:30)
Hail Mary...

Great crowds followed him, and he healed them there. (Matt 19:2)
Hail Mary...

Going out, he saw a great multitude, and he took pity on them, and he cured their sick. (Matt 14:14)
Hail Mary...

I will close up your scar, and I will heal you of your wounds, says the Lord. (Jer 30:17)
Hail Mary...

Jesus said to them: "This sickness is not unto death, but for the glory of God, so that the Son of God may be glorified by it." (Jn 11:4)
Hail Mary...

Jesus of Nazareth, whom God anointed with the Holy Spirit and with power, traveled around doing good and healing all those oppressed by the devil. For God was with him. (Acts 10:38)
Hail Mary...

They will turn to him, and he will hear their prayers and heal them. (Is 19:22, GNT)

Hail Mary...

Prayer made in faith will heal the sick; the Lord will restore them to health, and the sins they have committed will be forgiven. So then, confess your sins to one another and pray for one another, so that you will be healed. (Jas 5:15-16, GNT)
Hail Mary...

In your infirmity, you should not neglect yourself, but pray to the Lord, and he will cure you. (Sir 38:9)
Hail Mary...

He himself bore our sins in his body upon the tree, so that we, having died to sin, would live for justice. By his wounds, you have been healed. (1 Pet 2:24)
Hail Mary...

Glory Be...

Decade 3

Our Father...

Having called together his twelve disciples, he gave them authority over unclean spirits, to cast them out and to cure every sickness and every infirmity. (Matt 10:1)
Hail Mary...

Crowds of people came in from the towns around Jerusalem, bringing those who were sick or who had evil spirits in them; and they were all healed. (Acts 5:16, GNT)
Hail Mary...

They had come to hear him and to be healed of their diseases. Those who were troubled by evil spirits also came and were healed. (Luk 6:18, GNT)
Hail Mary...

The news about him spread through the whole country of Syria, so that people brought to him all those who were sick, suffering from all kinds of diseases and disorders: people with demons, and epileptics, and paralytics—and Jesus healed them all. (Matt 4:24, GNT)
Hail Mary...

The news about Jesus spread all the more widely, and crowds of people came to hear him and be healed from their diseases. (Luk 5:15, GNT)
Hail Mary...

The people were amazed as they saw the dumb speaking, the crippled made whole, the lame walking, and the blind seeing; and they praised the God of Israel. (Matt 15:31, GNT)
Hail Mary...

The entire crowd was trying to touch him, because power went out from him and healed all. (Luk 6:19)
Hail Mary...

Is anyone ill among you? Let him bring in the priests of the Church, and let them pray over him, anointing him with oil in the name of the Lord. (Jas 5:14)
Hail Mary...

I have seen their ways, but I will heal them; I will lead them and repay them with comfort, creating for their mourners the fruit of the lips. Peace, peace, to the far and the near, says the Lord; and I will heal them. (Is 57:18-19, NRSVCE)
Hail Mary...

Behold, I will lead over them scars and health, and I will cure them. And I will reveal to them an invocation of peace and truth. (Jer 33:6)
Hail Mary...

Glory Be...

Decade 4

Our Father...

In the church God has put all in place: in the first place apostles, in the second place prophets, and in the third place teachers; then those who perform miracles, followed by those who are given the power to heal or to help others or to direct them or to speak in strange tongues. (1 Cor 12:28 GNT)
Hail Mary...

They said to him, "Lord, let our eyes be opened." Moved with compassion, Jesus touched their eyes. Immediately they regained their sight and followed him. (Matt 20:33-34, NRSVCE)
Hail Mary...

The Lord sustains them on their sickbed; in their illness you heal all their infirmities. (Ps 41:3, NRSVCE)
Hail Mary...

Be gracious to me, O Lord, for I am languishing; O Lord, heal me, for my bones are shaking with terror. (Ps 6:2, NRSVCE)
Hail Mary...

The Spirit of the Lord is upon me; because of this, he has anointed me. He has sent me to evangelize the poor, to heal the contrite of heart. (Luk 4:18)
Hail Mary...

As for me, I said, "O Lord, be gracious to me; heal me, for I have sinned against you."(Ps 41:4, NRSVCE)
Hail Mary...

The crowds paid close attention to what Philip said, as they listened to him and saw the miracles that he performed. Evil spirits came out from many people with a loud cry, and many paralyzed and lame people were healed. (Acts 8:6-7, GNT)
Hail Mary...

Some people brought to Jesus a man who was blind and could not talk because he had a demon. Jesus healed the man, so that he was able to talk and see. (Matt 12:22, GNT)
Hail Mary...

He said to her: "Daughter, your faith has saved you. Go in peace, and be healed from your wound." (Mrk 5:34)
Hail Mary...

In whichever place he entered, in towns or villages or cities, they placed the infirm in the main streets, and they pleaded with him that they might touch even the hem of his garment. And as many as touched him were made healthy. (Mrk 6:56)
Hail Mary...

Glory Be...

Decade 5

Our Father...

When she had heard of Jesus, she approached through the crowd behind him, and she touched his garment. For she said: "Because if I touch even his garment, I will be saved." And immediately, the source of her bleeding was dried up, and she sensed in her body that she had been healed from the wound. (Mrk 5:27-29)
Hail Mary...

The Lord watches over those who love him; he is their strong protection and firm support. He shelters them from the heat, shades them from the noonday sun, and keeps them from stumbling and falling. He makes them cheerful and puts a sparkle in their eyes. He blesses them with life and health. (Sir 34:16-17, GNT)
Hail Mary...

Lord, I will live for you, for you alone; Heal me and let me live. (Is 38:16, GNT)
Hail Mary...

He gives power to the faint, and strengthens the powerless. Even youths will faint and be weary, and the young will fall exhausted; but those who wait for the Lord shall renew their strength. (Is 40:29-31, NRSVCE)
Hail Mary...

He heals the brokenhearted, and binds up their wounds. (Ps 147:3, NRSVCE)
Hail Mary...

My flesh and my heart may fail, but God is the strength of my heart and my portion forever. (Ps 73:26, NRSVCE)
Hail Mary...

God's works will never be finished; and from him health spreads over all the earth. (Sir 38:8, NRSVCE)
Hail Mary...

It was the power of his name that gave strength to this lame man. What you see and know was done by faith in his name; it was faith in Jesus that has made him well, as you can all see. (Acts 3:16, GNT)
Hail Mary...

God was accomplishing powerful and uncommon miracles by the hand of Paul, so much so that even when small cloths and wrappings were brought from his body to the sick, the illnesses withdrew from them and the wicked spirits departed. (Acts 19:11-12)
Hail Mary...

He found there a certain man, named Aeneas, who was a paralytic, who had lain in bed for eight years. And Peter said to him: "Aeneas, the Lord Jesus Christ heals you. Rise up and arrange your bed." And immediately he rose up. (Acts 9:33-34)
Hail Mary...

Glory Be…

Finances

Decade 1

Our Father…

Trust in the Lord, and do good; so you will live in the land, and enjoy security. Take delight in the Lord, and he will give you the desires of your heart. (Ps 37:3-4, NRSVCE)
Hail Mary…

Keep your lives free from the love of money, and be satisfied with what you have. For God has said, "I will never leave you; I will never abandon you." (Heb 13:5, GNT)
Hail Mary…

There is great gain in godliness combined with contentment; for we brought nothing into the world, so that we can take nothing out of it; but if we have food and clothing, we will be content with these. (1 Tim 6:6-8, NRSVCE)
Hail Mary…

Those who want to get rich fall into temptation and are caught in the trap of many foolish and harmful desires, which pull them down to ruin and destruction. For the love of money is a source of all kinds of evil. Some have been so eager to have it that they have wandered away from the faith and have broken their hearts with many sorrows. (1 Tim 6:9-10, GNT)
Hail Mary…

Instruct the wealthy of this age not to have a superior attitude, nor to hope in the uncertainty of riches, but in the living God, who offers us everything in abundance to enjoy. (1 Tim 6:17)
Hail Mary…

Blessed is the man who trusts in the Lord, for the Lord will be his confidence. And he will be like a tree planted beside waters, which sends out its roots to moist soil. And it will not fear when the heat arrives. And its leaves will be green. And in the time of drought, it will not be anxious, nor will it cease at any time to bear fruit. (Jer 17:7-8)
Hail Mary…

In you our ancestors trusted; they trusted, and you delivered them. To you they cried, and were saved; in you they trusted, and were not put to shame. (Ps 22:4-5, NRSVCE)
Hail Mary...

What do you have that you have not received? But if you have received it, why do you glory, as if you had not received it? (1 Cor 4:7)
Hail Mary...

O Jerusalem, you suffering, helpless city, with no one to comfort you, I will rebuild your foundations with precious stones. I will build your towers with rubies, your gates with stones that glow like fire, and the wall around you with jewels. (Is 54:11-12, GNT)
Hail Mary...

Stay with the Lord; never abandon him, and you will be prosperous at the end of your days. (Sir 2:3, GNT)
Hail Mary...

Glory Be...

Decade 2

Our Father...

No one is able to serve two masters. For either he will have hatred for the one, and love the other, or he will persevere with the one, and despise the other. You cannot serve God and wealth. (Matt 6:24)
Hail Mary...

Do not worry about tomorrow; it will have enough worries of its own. There is no need to add to the troubles each day brings. (Matt 6:34, GNT)
Hail Mary...

Sell what you possess, and give alms. Make for yourselves purses that will not wear out, a treasure that will not fall short, in heaven, where no thief approaches, and no moth corrupts. For where your treasure is, there will your heart be also. (Luk 12:33-34)
Hail Mary...

I will repay you for the years which the locust, and the beetle, and the mildew, and the caterpillar consumed: my great strength which I sent

upon you. And you will eat with enjoyment, and you will be satisfied, and you will praise the name of the Lord your God, who has worked miracles with you. (Joel 2:25-26)
Hail Mary...

I have learned to be content with whatever I have. I know what it is to have little, and I know what it is to have plenty. In any and all circumstances I have learned the secret of being well-fed and of going hungry, of having plenty and of being in need. (Phil 4:11-12, NRSVCE)
Hail Mary...

My God will fully satisfy every need of yours according to his riches in glory in Christ Jesus. (Phil 4:19, NRSVCE)
Hail Mary...

If you obey God and avoid sin, he will be pleased with you and make you prosperous. (Tob 4:21, GNT)
Hail Mary...

The Lord your God has blessed you in every work of your hands. The Lord your God, dwelling with you, knows your journey, how you crossed through this great wilderness over forty years, and how you have been lacking in nothing. (Deut 2:7)
Hail Mary...

During these forty years your clothes have not worn out, nor have your feet swollen up. Remember that the Lord your God corrects and punishes you just as parents discipline their children. So then, do as the Lord has commanded you: live according to his laws and obey him. (Deut 8:4-6, GNT)
Hail Mary...

The Lord your God is bringing you into a fertile land—a land that has rivers and springs, and underground streams gushing out into the valleys and hills; a land that produces wheat and barley, grapes, figs, pomegranates, olives, and honey. There you will never go hungry or ever be in need. (Deut 8:7-9, GNT)
Hail Mary...

Glory Be...

Decade 3

Our Father...

Remember that it is the Lord your God who gives you the power to become rich. He does this because he is still faithful today to the covenant that he made with your ancestors. (Deut 8:18, GNT)
Hail Mary...

Bring all the tithes into the storehouse, and let there be food in my house. And test me about this, says the Lord, as to whether I will not open to you the floodgates of heaven, and pour out to you a blessing, all the way to abundance. (Mal 3:10)
Hail Mary...

I have been young, and now am old, yet I have not seen the righteous forsaken or their children begging bread. They are ever giving liberally and lending, and their children become a blessing. (Ps 37:25-26, NRSVCE)
Hail Mary...

He will love you and multiply you. And he will bless the fruit of your womb, and the fruit of your land: your grain as well as your vintage, oil, and herds, and the flocks of your sheep, upon the land about which he swore to your fathers that he would give it to you. (Deut 7:13)
Hail Mary...

Give your help to the poor, and the Lord will give you his perfect blessing. (Sir 7:32, GNT)
Hail Mary...

I will rebuke for your sakes the devourer, and he will not corrupt the fruit of your land. Neither will the vine in the field be barren, says the Lord of hosts. (Mal 3:11)
Hail Mary...

If my people who are called by my name humble themselves, pray, seek my face, and turn from their wicked ways, then I will hear from heaven, and will forgive their sin and heal their land. (2 Chron 7:13-14, NRSVCE)
Hail Mary...

The Lord their God will be mindful of them and restore their fortunes. (Zeph 2:7, NRSVCE)
Hail Mary...

The time is coming! I will bring your scattered people home; I will make you famous throughout the world and make you prosperous once again.(Zeph 3:20, GNT)
Hail Mary...

Return, you exiles who now have hope; return to your place of safety. Now I tell you that I will repay you twice over with blessing for all you have suffered. (Zech 9:12, GNT)
Hail Mary...

Glory Be...

Decade 4

Our Father...

God, who supplies seed for the sower and bread to eat, will also supply you with all the seed you need and will make it grow and produce a rich harvest from your generosity. (2 Cor 9:10, GNT)
Hail Mary...

You will be enriched in every way for your great generosity, which will produce thanksgiving to God through us. (2 Cor 9:11, NRSVCE)
Hail Mary...

I will bring my people back to their land. They will rebuild their ruined cities and live there; they will plant vineyards and drink the wine; they will plant gardens and eat what they grow. I will plant my people on the land I gave them, and they will not be pulled up again. (Amos 9:14-15, GNT)
Hail Mary...

I will restore them to the land which I pledged to their fathers, Abraham, Isaac, and Jacob, and they will rule over it, and I will multiply them, and they will not be diminished. (Bar 2:34)
Hail Mary...

I will save you from all your filth. And I will call for grain, and I will multiply it, and I will not impose a famine upon you. And I will multiply the fruit of the tree and the produce of the field, so that you may no longer bear the disgrace of famine among the nations. (Eze 36:29-30)
Hail Mary...

God gives the desolate a home to live in; he leads out the prisoners to prosperity. (Ps 68:6, NRSVCE)
Hail Mary...

Rain in abundance, O God, you showered abroad; you restored your heritage when it languished; your flock found a dwelling in it; in your goodness, O God, you provided for the needy. (Ps 68:9-10, NRSVCE)
Hail Mary...

The Lord will send forth a blessing upon your cellars, and upon all the works of your hands. And he will bless you in the land that you shall receive. (Deut 28:8)
Hail Mary...

Honor the Lord with your substance, and give to him from the first of all your fruits, and then your storehouses will be filled with abundance, and your presses shall overflow with wine. (Pro 3:9-10)
Hail Mary...

Do not choose to be anxious, saying: 'What shall we eat, and what shall we drink, and with what shall we be clothed?' For the Gentiles seek all these things. Yet your Father knows that you need all these things. (Matt 6:31-32)
Hail Mary...

Glory Be...

Decade 5

Our Father...

May the Lord give you increase, both you and your children. May you be blessed by the Lord, who made heaven and earth. (Ps 115:14-15, NRSVCE)
Hail Mary...

The young lions suffer want and hunger, but those who seek the Lord lack no good thing. (Ps 34:10, NRSVCE)
Hail Mary...

The blessing of the Lord causes riches. Affliction will not be a companion to them. (Pro 10:22)
Hail Mary...

You open your hand, satisfying the desire of every living thing. (Ps 145:16, NRSVCE)
Hail Mary…

The Lord will cause you to be abundant in every good thing: in the fruit of your womb, and in the fruit of your cattle, and in the fruit of your land, which the Lord swore to your fathers that he would give to you. (Deut 28:11)
Hail Mary…

The Lord will open his excellent treasury, the heavens, so that it may distribute rain in due time. And he will bless all the works of your hands. And you shall lend to many nations, but you yourself will borrow nothing from anyone. (Deut 28:12)
Hail Mary…

If only they would always feel this way! If only they would always honor me and obey all my commands, so that everything would go well with them and their descendants forever. (Deut 5:29, GNT)
Hail Mary…

Whoever trusts in his riches will fall. But the just shall spring up like a green leaf. (Pro 11:28)
Hail Mary…

The Lord was moved by the repentance of Job, when he prayed for his friends. And the Lord gave to Job twice as much as he had before. (Job 42:10)
Hail Mary…

God is able to make every grace abound in you, so that, always having what you need in all things, you may abound unto every good work. (2 Cor 9:8)
Hail Mary…

Glory Be…

God's Love

Decade 1

Our Father...

God so loved the world that he gave his only-begotten Son, so that all who believe in him may not perish, but may have eternal life. (Jn 3:16)
Hail Mary...

The mountains may depart and the hills be removed, but my steadfast love shall not depart from you. (Is 54:10, NRSVCE)
Hail Mary...

I have loved you with an everlasting love; therefore I have continued my faithfulness to you. (Jer 31:3, NRSVCE)
Hail Mary...

The steadfast love of the Lord never ceases, his mercies never come to an end; they are new every morning; great is your faithfulness. (Lam 3:22, NRSVCE)
Hail Mary...

God's love has been poured into our hearts through the Holy Spirit that has been given to us. (Rom 5:5, NRSVCE)
Hail Mary...

God has shown us how much he loves us — it was while we were still sinners that Christ died for us! (Rom 5:8, GNT)
Hail Mary...

Because your steadfast love is better than life, my lips will praise you. So I will bless you as long as I live; I will lift up my hands and call on your name. (Ps 63:3-4, NRSVCE)
Hail Mary...

I am certain that neither death, nor life, nor Angels, nor Principalities, nor Powers, nor the present things, nor the future things, nor strength, nor the heights, nor the depths, nor any other created thing, will be able to separate us from the love of God, which is in Christ Jesus our Lord. (Rom 8:38-39)
Hail Mary...

God's mercy is so abundant, and his love for us is so great, that while we were spiritually dead in our disobedience he brought us to life with Christ. It is by God's grace that you have been saved. (Eph 2:4-5, GNT)

Hail Mary...

For through the law, I have become dead to the law, so that I may live for God. I have been nailed to the cross with Christ. I live; yet now, it is not I, but truly Christ, who lives in me. And though I live now in the flesh, I live in the faith of the Son of God, who loved me and who delivered himself for me. (Gal 2:19-20)

Hail Mary...

Glory Be...

Decade 2

Our Father...

See how much the Father has loved us! His love is so great that we are called God's children—and so, in fact, we are. This is why the world does not know us: it has not known God. (1 Jn 3:1, GNT)

Hail Mary...

Truly the eye of the Lord is on those who fear him, on those who hope in his steadfast love, to deliver their soul from death, and to keep them alive in famine. (Ps 33:18-19, NRSVCE)

Hail Mary...

How precious is your steadfast love, O God! All people may take refuge in the shadow of your wings. (Ps 36:7, NRSVCE)

Hail Mary...

The Lord your God is with you; his power gives you victory. The Lord will take delight in you, and in his love he will give you new life. (Zeph 3:17, GNT)

Hail Mary...

Many are the torments of the wicked, but steadfast love surrounds those who trust in the Lord. (Ps 32:10, NRSVCE)

Hail Mary...

This is what love is: it is not that we have loved God, but that he loved us and sent his Son to be the means by which our sins are forgiven. (1 Jn 4:10, GNT)
Hail Mary...

Let us love God, for God first loved us. (1 Jn 4:19)
Hail Mary...

I in them and you in me, so that they may be completely one, in order that the world may know that you sent me and that you love them as you love me. (Jn 17:23, GNT)
Hail Mary...

I will be true and faithful; I will show you constant love and mercy and make you mine forever. I will keep my promise and make you mine, and you will acknowledge me as Lord. (Hos 2:19-20, GNT)
Hail Mary...

I was the one who taught Israel to walk. I took my people up in my arms, but they did not acknowledge that I took care of them. I drew them to me with affection and love. I picked them up and held them to my cheek; I bent down to them and fed them. (Hos 11:3-4, GNT)
Hail Mary...

Glory Be...

Decade 3

Our Father...

If my father and mother forsake me, the Lord will take me up. (Ps 27:10, NRSVCE)
Hail Mary...

I will give up whole nations to save your life, because you are precious to me and because I love you and give you honor. (Is 43:4, GNT)
Hail Mary...

Can a woman forget her infant, so as not to take pity on the child of her womb? But even if she would forget, still I shall never forget you. (Is 49:15)
Hail Mary...

For a brief moment, I have forsaken you, and with great pities, I will gather you. In a moment of indignation, I have hidden my face from you, for a little while. But with everlasting mercy, I have taken pity on you, said your Redeemer, the Lord. (Is 54:7-8)
Hail Mary...

Even the very hairs of your head have all been numbered. Therefore, do not be afraid. You are worth more than many sparrows. (Luk 12:7)
Hail Mary...

You are a gracious God and merciful, slow to anger, and abounding in steadfast love, and ready to relent from punishing. (Jon 4:2, NRSVCE)
Hail Mary...

Behold, I have engraved you on my hands. Your walls are always before my eyes. (Is 49:16)
Hail Mary...

Consider the birds of the air, how they neither sow, nor reap, nor gather into barns, and yet your heavenly Father feeds them. Are you not of much greater value than they are? (Matt 6:26)
Hail Mary...

My child, do not despise the Lord's discipline or be weary of his reproof, for the Lord reproves the one he loves, as a father the son in whom he delights. (Pro 3:11-12, NRSVCE)
Hail Mary...

What are human beings that you are mindful of them, mortals that you care for them? Yet you have made them a little lower than God, and crowned them with glory and honor. (Ps 8:4-5, NRSVCE)
Hail Mary...

Glory Be...

Decade 4

Our Father...

My child, pay attention when the Lord corrects you, and do not be discouraged when he rebukes you. Because the Lord corrects everyone he loves, and punishes everyone he accepts as a child. (Heb 12:5-6, GNT)
Hail Mary...

I will bring my people back to me. I will love them with all my heart; no longer am I angry with them. (Hos 14:4)
Hail Mary...

The virgin will rejoice with singing, the young and the old together, and I will turn their mourning into gladness, and I will console them and gladden them after their sorrow. (Jer 31:13)
Hail Mary...

I will satisfy the weary, and all who are faint I will replenish. (Jer 31:25, NRSVCE)
Hail Mary...

I alone know the plans I have for you, plans to bring you prosperity and not disaster, plans to bring about the future you hope for. (Jer 29:11, GNT)
Hail Mary...

Rising up, he went to his father. But while he was still at a distance, his father saw him, and he was moved with compassion, and running to him, he fell upon his neck and kissed him. (Luk 15:20)
Hail Mary...

I passed by you and saw you. And behold, your time was the time of lovers. And I spread my garment over you, and I covered your disgrace. And I swore to you, and I entered into a covenant with you, says the Lord God, and you became mine. (Eze 16:8)
Hail Mary...

I will remember my covenant with you in the days of your youth. And I will raise up for you an everlasting covenant. (Eze 16:60)
Hail Mary...

Thus says the Lord who created you, O Jacob, and who formed you, O Israel: Do not be afraid. For I have redeemed you, and I have called you by your name. You are mine. (Is 43:1)
Hail Mary...

When you pass through the waters, I will be with you, and the rivers will not cover you. When you walk through fire, you will not be burned, and the flames will not scorch you. (Is 43:2)
Hail Mary...

Glory Be...

Decade 5

Our Father...

Your eyes beheld my unformed substance. In your book were written all the days that were formed for me. (Ps 139:16, NRSVCE)
Hail Mary...

When the kindness and love of God our Savior was revealed, he saved us. It was not because of any good deeds that we ourselves had done, but because of his own mercy that he saved us, through the Holy Spirit, who gives us new birth and new life by washing us. (Tit 3:4-5, GNT)
Hail Mary...

The love of God was made apparent to us in this way: that God sent his only-begotten Son into the world, so that we might live through him. (1 Jn 4:9)
Hail Mary...

He who did not withhold his own Son, but gave him up for all of us, will he not with him also give us everything else? (Rom 8:32, NRSVCE)
Hail Mary...

I pray that Christ will make his home in your hearts through faith. I pray that you may have your roots and foundation in love, so that you, together with all God's people, may have the power to understand how broad and long, how high and deep, is Christ's love. (Eph 3:17-18, GNT)
Hail Mary...

The Lord is waiting to be merciful to you. He is ready to take pity on you because he always does what is right. Happy are those who put their trust in the Lord. (Is 30:18, GNT)
Hail Mary...

The Lord will never give up his mercy, or cause any of his works to perish; he will never blot out the descendants of his chosen one, or destroy the family line of him who loved him. (Sir 47:22, NRSVCE)
Hail Mary...

The eye has not seen, and the ear has not heard, nor has it entered into the heart of man, what things God has prepared for those who love him. (1 Cor 2:9)

Hail Mary...

The Lord is my shepherd, I shall not want. He makes me lie down in green pastures; he leads me beside still waters; he restores my soul. (Ps 23:1-3, NRSVCE)
Hail Mary...

Let your steadfast love become my comfort according to your promise to your servant. (Ps 119:76, NRSVCE)
Hail Mary...

Glory Be...

Love for Neighbor

Decade 1

Our Father...

You are the people of God; he loved you and chose you for his own. So then, you must clothe yourselves with compassion, kindness, humility, gentleness, and patience. (Col 3:12, GNT)
Hail Mary...

Be tolerant with one another and forgive one another whenever any of you has a complaint against someone else. You must forgive one another just as the Lord has forgiven you. (Col 3:13, GNT)
Hail Mary...

Above all, clothe yourselves with love, which binds everything together in perfect harmony. (Col 3:14, NRSVCE)
Hail Mary...

Be angry, but do not be willing to sin. Do not let the sun set over your anger. Provide no place for the devil. (Eph 4:26-27)
Hail Mary...

When we are cursed, we bless; when we are persecuted, we endure; when we are insulted, we answer back with kind words. (1 Cor 4:12-13, GNT)
Hail Mary...

Love is patient and kind; it is not jealous or conceited or proud; love is not ill-mannered or selfish or irritable; love does not keep a record of wrongs; love is not happy with evil, but is happy with the truth. Love never gives up; and its faith, hope, and patience never fail. (1 Cor 13:4-7, GNT)
Hail Mary...

I may have the gift of inspired preaching; I may have all knowledge and understand all secrets; I may have all the faith needed to move mountains—but if I have no love, I am nothing. I may give away everything I have, and even give up my body to be burned—but if I have no love, this does me no good. (1 Cor 13:2-3, GNT)
Hail Mary...

If anyone says that he loves God, but hates his brother, then he is a liar. For he who does not love his brother, whom he does see, in what way can he love God, whom he does not see? (1 Jn 4:20)
Hail Mary...

Peter came to Jesus and asked, "Lord, if my brother keeps on sinning against me, how many times do I have to forgive him? Seven times?" "No, not seven times," answered Jesus, "but seventy times seven." (Matt 18:21-22, GNT)
Hail Mary...

No one has a greater love than this: that he lay down his life for his friends. (Jn 15:13)
Hail Mary...

Glory Be...

Decade 2

Our Father...

If you offer your gift at the altar, and there you remember that your brother has something against you, leave your gift there, before the altar, and go first to be reconciled to your brother, and then you may approach and offer your gift. (Matt 5:23-24)
Hail Mary...

Love your enemies and pray for those who persecute you, so that you may become the children of your Father in heaven. (Matt 5:44, GNT)
Hail Mary...

I give you a new commandment: Love one another. Just as I have loved you, so also must you love one another. By this, all shall recognize that you are my disciples: if you will have love for one another. (Jn 13:34-35)
Hail Mary...

If we say that we are in the light, yet hate others, we are in the darkness to this very hour. If we love others, we live in the light, and so there is nothing in us that will cause someone else to sin. (1 Jn 2:9-10, GNT)
Hail Mary...

We know that we have left death and come over into life; we know it because we love others. Those who do not love are still under the power of death. (1 Jn 3:14, GNT)
Hail Mary...

Those who hate others are murderers, and you know that murderers do not have eternal life in them. (1 Jn 3:15, GNT)
Hail Mary...

You must all have the same attitude and the same feelings; love one another, and be kind and humble with one another. Do not pay back evil with evil or cursing with cursing; instead, pay back with a blessing, because a blessing is what God promised to give you when he called you. (1 Pet 3:8-9, GNT)
Hail Mary...

Love must be completely sincere. Hate what is evil, hold on to what is good. Love one another warmly as Christians, and be eager to show respect for one another. (Rom 12:9-10, GNT)
Hail Mary...

Never take revenge, my friends, but instead let God's anger do it. For the scripture says, "I will take revenge, I will pay back, says the Lord." Instead, as the scripture says: "If your enemies are hungry, feed them; if they are thirsty, give them a drink; for by doing this you will make them burn with shame." Do not let evil defeat you; instead, conquer evil with good. (Rom 12:19-21, GNT)
Hail Mary...

Do to others as you would have them do to you. (Luk 6:31, NRSVCE)
Hail Mary...

Glory Be...

Decade 3

Our Father...

Love your enemies and do good to them; lend and expect nothing back. You will then have a great reward, and you will be children of the Most High God. For he is good to the ungrateful and the wicked. (Luk 6:35, GNT)
Hail Mary...

This is my precept: that you love one another, just as I have loved you. (Jn 15:12)
Hail Mary...

This is love: that we walk according to his commandments. For this is the commandment that you have heard in the same way from the beginning, and in which you should walk. (2 Jn 1:6)
Hail Mary...

Do for others what you want them to do for you: this is the meaning of the Law of Moses and of the teachings of the prophets. (Matt 7:12, GNT)
Hail Mary...

Most beloved, let us love one another. For love is of God. (1 Jn 4:7)
Hail Mary...

Everyone who loves is born of God and knows God. Whoever does not love, does not know God. For God is love. (1 Jn 4:8)
Hail Mary...

Now that by your obedience to the truth you have purified yourselves and have come to have a sincere love for other believers, love one another earnestly with all your heart. (1 Pet 1:22, GNT)
Hail Mary...

Be always humble, gentle, and patient. Show your love by being tolerant with one another. Do your best to preserve the unity which the Spirit gives by means of the peace that binds you together. (Eph 4:2-3)
Hail Mary...

Above all, maintain constant love for one another, for love covers a multitude of sins. Be hospitable to one another without complaining. (1 Pet 4:8-9, NRSVCE)
Hail Mary...

You should owe nothing to anyone, except so as to love one another. For whoever loves his neighbor has fulfilled the law. (Rom 13:8)
Hail Mary...

Glory Be...

Decade 4

Our Father…

This is his commandment: that we should believe in the name of his Son, Jesus Christ, and love one another, just as he has commanded us. (1 Jn 3:23)
Hail Mary…

When you stand to pray, if you hold anything against anyone, forgive them, so that your Father, who is in heaven, may also forgive you your sins. (Mrk 11:25)
Hail Mary…

My children, our love should not be just words and talk; it must be true love, which shows itself in action. (1 Jn 3:18, GNT)
Hail Mary…

Whoever possesses the goods of this world, and sees his brother to be in need, and yet closes his heart to him: in what way does the love of God abide in him? (1 Jn 3:17)
Hail Mary…

Let all that you do be done in love. (1 Cor 16:13, NRSVCE)
Hail Mary…

'You shall love the Lord your God from all your heart, and with all your soul and with all your mind.' This is the greatest and first commandment. But the second is similar to it: 'You shall love your neighbor as yourself.' On these two commandments the entire law depends, and also the prophets. (Matt 22:37-40)
Hail Mary…

You were called to freedom, brothers and sisters; only do not use your freedom as an opportunity for self-indulgence, but through love become slaves to one another. (Gal 5:14, NRSVCE)
Hail Mary…

No one has ever seen God. But if we love one another, God abides in us, and his love is perfected in us. (1 Jn 4:12)
Hail Mary…

This is how we know what love is: Christ gave his life for us. We too, then, ought to give our lives for others! (1 Jn 3:16, GNT)

Hail Mary...

Forgive your neighbor, if he has harmed you, and then your sins will be forgiven you when you pray. (Sir 28:2)
Hail Mary...

Glory Be...

Decade 5

Our Father...

If you will forgive men their sins, your heavenly Father also will forgive you your offenses. But if you will not forgive men, neither will your Father forgive you your sins. (Matt 6:14-15)
Hail Mary...

You do well if you really fulfill the royal law according to the scripture, "You shall love your neighbor as yourself." (Jas 2:8, NRSVCE)
Hail Mary...

In this way, the sons of God are made manifest, and also the sons of the devil. Everyone who is not just, is not of God, as also anyone who does not love his brother. (1 Jn 3:10)
Hail Mary...

You shall not commit adultery. You shall not kill. You shall not steal. You shall not speak false testimony. You shall not covet. And if there is any other commandment, it is summed up in this word: You shall love your neighbor as yourself. (Rom 13:9)
Hail Mary...

Let mutual love continue. Do not neglect to show hospitality to strangers, for by doing that some have entertained angels without knowing it. (Heb 13:1-2, NRSVCE)
Hail Mary...

Therefore, while we have time, we should do good works toward everyone, and most of all toward those who are of the household of the faith. (Gal 6:10)
Hail Mary...

Carry one another's burdens, and so shall you fulfill the law of Christ. (Gal 6:2)
Hail Mary...

You must love God with all your heart and with all your mind and with all your strength; and you must love your neighbor as you love yourself. It is more important to obey these two commandments than to offer on the altar animals and other sacrifices to God. (Mrk 12:33, GNT)

Hail Mary...

Let all bitterness and anger and indignation and outcry and blasphemy be taken away from you, along with all malice. And be kind and merciful to one another, forgiving one another, just as God has forgiven you in Christ. (Eph 4:31-32)

Hail Mary...

Blessed are the merciful, for they shall obtain mercy. (Matt 5:7)

Hail Mary...

Glory Be...

The Holy Spirit

Decade 1

Our Father…

Ask, and it shall be given to you. Seek, and you shall find. Knock, and it shall be opened to you. For everyone who asks, receives; and whoever seeks, finds; and to anyone who knocks, it will be opened. (Matt 7:7-8)
Hail Mary…

My Spirit is within you, and my words, which I have put in your mouth, will not withdraw from your mouth, nor from the mouth of your offspring, nor from the mouth of your offspring's offspring, says the Lord, from this moment, and even forever. (Is 59:21)
Hail Mary…

The Helper, the Holy Spirit, whom the Father will send in my name, will teach you everything and make you remember all that I have told you. (Jn 14:26, GNT)
Hail Mary…

When the Spirit of truth has arrived, he will teach the whole truth to you. For he will not be speaking from himself. Instead, whatever he will hear, he will speak. And he will announce to you the things that are to come. (Jn 16:13)
Hail Mary…

When the Holy Spirit comes upon you, you will be filled with power, and you will be witnesses for me in Jerusalem, in all of Judea and Samaria, and to the ends of the earth. (Acts 1:8, GNT)
Hail Mary…

Let anyone who is thirsty come to me, and let the one who believes in me drink. As the scripture has said, 'Out of the believer's heart shall flow rivers of living water.' (Jn 7:37-38, NRSVCE)
Hail Mary…

Those who drink the water that I will give them will never be thirsty again. The water that I will give them will become in them a spring

which will provide them with life-giving water and give them eternal life. (Jn 4:14, GNT)
Hail Mary...

I pray that, according to the riches of his glory, he may grant that you may be strengthened in your inner being with power through his Spirit. (Eph 3:16, NRSVCE)
Hail Mary...

Not by might, nor by power, but by my spirit, says the Lord of hosts. (Zech 4:6, NRSVCE)
Hail Mary...

No one has ever learned your will, unless you first gave him wisdom, and sent your Holy Spirit down to him. (Wis 9:17, GNT)
Hail Mary...

Glory Be...

Decade 2

Our Father...

The Spirit helps us in our weakness; for we do not know how to pray as we ought, but that very Spirit intercedes with sighs too deep for words. (Rom 8:26, NRSVCE)
Hail Mary...

He who examines hearts knows what the Spirit seeks, because he asks on behalf of the saints in accordance with God. (Rom 8:27)
Hail Mary...

Those who are in agreement with the flesh are mindful of the things of the flesh. But those who are in agreement with the spirit are mindful of the things of the spirit. (Rom 8:5)
Hail Mary...

To set the mind on the flesh is death, but to set the mind on the Spirit is life and peace. (Rom 8:6, NRSVCE)
Hail Mary...

If the Spirit of him who raised up Jesus from the dead lives within you, then he who raised up Jesus Christ from the dead shall also

enliven your mortal bodies, by means of his Spirit living within you. (Rom 8:11)
Hail Mary...

If you live according to the flesh, you will die. But if, by the Spirit, you mortify the deeds of the flesh, you shall live. (Rom 8:13)
Hail Mary...

Those who are led by God's Spirit are God's children. (Rom 8:14, GNT)
Hail Mary...

Do not get drunk with wine, which will only ruin you; instead, be filled with the Spirit. Speak to one another with the words of psalms, hymns, and sacred songs; sing hymns and psalms to the Lord with praise in your hearts. (Eph 5:18-19, GNT)
Hail Mary...

Anyone who will have spoken a word against the Son of man shall be forgiven. But whoever will have spoken against the Holy Spirit shall not be forgiven, neither in this age, nor in the future age. (Matt 12:32)
Hail Mary...

The Spirit of the Lord will rest upon him: the spirit of wisdom and understanding, the spirit of counsel and fortitude, the spirit of knowledge and piety. And he will be filled with the spirit of the fear of the Lord. He will not judge according to the sight of the eyes, nor reprove according to the hearing of the ears. (Is 11:2-3)
Hail Mary...

Glory Be...

Decade 3

Our Father...

Do not worry about what you are going to say or how you will say it; when the time comes, you will be given what you will say. For the words you will speak will not be yours; they will come from the Spirit of your Father speaking through you. (Matt 10:19-20, GNT)
Hail Mary...

No one speaking in the Spirit of God utters a curse against Jesus. And no one is able to say that Jesus is Lord, except in the Holy Spirit. (1 Cor 12:3)
Hail Mary...

Indeed, in one Spirit, we were all baptized into one body, whether Jews or Gentiles, whether servant or free. And we all drank in the one Spirit. (1 Cor 12:13)
Hail Mary...

Since you are eager for spiritual gifts, strive to excel in them for building up the church. (1 Cor 14:12, NRSVCE)
Hail Mary...

I will ask the Father, and he will give another advocate to you, so that he may abide with you for eternity. (Jn 14:16)
Hail Mary...

He is the Spirit, who reveals the truth about God. The world cannot receive him, because it cannot see him or know him. But you know him, because he remains with you and is in you. (Jn 14:17, GNT)
Hail Mary...

To show that you are his children, God sent the Spirit of his Son into our hearts, the Spirit who cries out, "Father, my Father." (Gal 4:6, GNT)
Hail Mary...

Walk in the spirit, and you will not fulfill the desires of the flesh. (Gal 5:16)
Hail Mary...

The fruit of the Spirit is love, joy, peace, patience, kindness, generosity, faithfulness, gentleness, and self-control. There is no law against such things. (Gal 5:22-23, GNT)
Hail Mary...

If we live by the Spirit, let us also be guided by the Spirit. (Gal 5:25, NRSVCE)
Hail Mary...

Glory Be...

Decade 4

Our Father...

If you sow to your own flesh, you will reap corruption from the flesh; but if you sow to the Spirit, you will reap eternal life from the Spirit. (Gal 6:8, NRSVCE)
Hail Mary...

Those who keep his commandments abide in him, and he in them. And we know that he abides in us by this: by the Spirit, whom he has given to us. (1 Jn 3:24)
Hail Mary...

We are sure that we live in union with God and that he lives in union with us, because he has given us his Spirit. (1 Jn 4:13, GNT)
Hail Mary...

The one whom God has sent speaks God's words, because God gives him the fullness of his Spirit. (Jn 3:34, GNT)
Hail Mary...

Pray in the Spirit at all times in every prayer and supplication. To that end keep alert and always persevere in supplication for all the saints. (Eph 6:18, NRSVCE)
Hail Mary...

Each one of you must turn away from your sins and be baptized in the name of Jesus Christ, so that your sins will be forgiven; and you will receive God's gift, the Holy Spirit. (Acts 2:38, GNT)
Hail Mary...

Do you not know that your bodies are the Temple of the Holy Spirit, who is in you, whom you have from God, and that you are not your own? For you have been bought at a great price. Glorify and carry God in your body. (1 Cor 6:19-20)
Hail Mary...

If you then, who are evil, know how to give good gifts to your children, how much more will the heavenly Father give the Holy Spirit to those who ask him! (Luk 11:13, NRSVCE)
Hail Mary...

Now the Spirit is Lord. And wherever the Spirit of the Lord is, there is liberty. (2 Cor 3:17)
Hail Mary...

It is better for you that I go away, because if I do not go, the Helper will not come to you. But if I do go away, then I will send him to you. And when he comes, he will prove to the people of the world that they are wrong about sin and about what is right and about God's judgment. (Jn 16:7-8, GNT)
Hail Mary...

Glory Be...

Decade 5

Our Father...

Do not grieve the Holy Spirit of God, with which you were marked with a seal for the day of redemption. (Eph 4:30, NRSVCE)
Hail Mary...

But as for you, let the Anointing that you have received from him abide in you. And so, you have no need of anyone to teach you. For his Anointing teaches you about everything, and it is the truth, and it is not a lie. And just as his Anointing has taught you, abide in him. (1 Jn 2:27)
Hail Mary...

May the God of hope fill you with every joy and with peace in believing, so that you may abound in hope and in the virtue of the Holy Spirit. (Rom 15:13)
Hail Mary...

I will put my spirit in you and will see to it that you follow my laws and keep all the commands I have given you. (Eze 36:27, GNT)
Hail Mary...

When they had prayed, the place in which they were gathered was moved. And they were all filled with the Holy Spirit. And they were speaking the Word of God with confidence. (Acts 4:31)
Hail Mary...

You are not in the flesh; you are in the Spirit, since the Spirit of God dwells in you. (Rom 8:9, NRSVCE)
Hail Mary...

This is what I will do in the last days, God says: I will pour out my Spirit on everyone. Your sons and daughters will proclaim my

message; your young men will see visions, and your old men will have dreams. (Acts 2:17, GNT)
Hail Mary...

God poured out the Holy Spirit abundantly on us through Jesus Christ our Savior, so that by his grace we might be put right with God and come into possession of the eternal life we hope for. (Tit 3:6-7, GNT)
Hail Mary...

We have not received the spirit of this world, but the Spirit who is of God, so that we may understand the things that have been given to us by God. (1 Cor 2:12)
Hail Mary...

The spirit of the Lord God is upon me, because the Lord has anointed me; he has sent me to bring good news to the oppressed, to bind up the brokenhearted, to proclaim liberty to the captives, and release to the prisoners. (Is 61:1, NRSVCE)
Hail Mary...

Glory Be...

Repentance

Decade 1

Our Father...

As I live, says the Lord God, I do not desire the death of the impious, but that the impious should convert from his way and live. Be converted, be converted from your evil ways! For why should you die, O house of Israel? (Eze 33:11)
Hail Mary...

"But even now," says the Lord, "repent sincerely and return to me with fasting and weeping and mourning." (Joel 2:12, GNT)
Hail Mary...

I will pour clean water over you, and you shall be cleansed from all your filth, and I will cleanse you from all your idols. And I will give to you a new heart, and I will place in you a new spirit. And I will take away the heart of stone from your body, and I will give to you a heart of flesh. (Eze 36:25-26)
Hail Mary...

The Lord is not delaying his promise, as some imagine, but he does act patiently for your sake, not wanting anyone to perish, but wanting all to be turned back to penance. (2 Pet 3:9)
Hail Mary...

"If someone evil stops sinning and keeps my laws, if he does what is right and good, he will not die; he will certainly live. All his sins will be forgiven, and he will live, because he did what is right. Do you think I enjoy seeing evil people die?" asks the Sovereign Lord. "No, I would rather see them repent and live." (Eze 18:21-23, GNT)
Hail Mary...

I will judge each one according to his ways, says the Lord God. Be converted, and do penance for all your iniquities, and then iniquity will not be your ruin. Cast all your transgressions, by which you have transgressed, away from you, and make for yourselves a new heart and a new spirit. And then why should you die, O house of Israel? For I do not desire the death of one who dies, says the Lord God. So return and live. (Eze 18:30-32)

Hail Mary...

I say to you, that there will be so much more joy in heaven over one sinner repenting, than over the ninety-nine just, who do not need to repent. (Luk 15:7)
Hail Mary...

Depart from evil, and do good; seek peace, and pursue it. (Ps 34:14, NRSVCE)
Hail Mary...

Jesus answered, "Those who are well have no need of a physician, but those who are sick; I have come to call not the righteous but sinners to repentance." (Luk 5:31-32, NRSVCE)
Hail Mary...

Change the way you are living and stop doing the things you are doing. Be fair in your treatment of one another. Stop taking advantage of aliens, orphans, and widows. Stop killing innocent people in this land. Stop worshiping other gods, for that will destroy you. If you change, I will let you go on living here in the land which I gave your ancestors as a permanent possession. (Jer 7:5-7, GNT)
Hail Mary...

Glory Be...

Decade 2

Our Father...

Come to the Lord, and leave your sin behind. Pray sincerely that he will help you live a better life. Return to the Most High and turn away from sin. Have an intense hatred for wickedness. (Sir 17:25-26, GNT)
Hail Mary...

Wash, become clean, take away the evil of your intentions from my eyes. Cease to act perversely. (Is 1:16)
Hail Mary...

Thus says the Lord of hosts, the God of Israel: Make your ways and your intentions good, and I will live with you in this place. (Jer 7:3)
Hail Mary...

Turn now, every one of you, from your evil way and wicked doings, and you will remain upon the land that the Lord has given to you and your ancestors from of old and forever. (Jer 25:4, NRSVCE)
Hail Mary...

If they repent with all their heart and soul in the land of their captivity, to which they were taken captive, and pray toward their land, which you gave to their ancestors, the city that you have chosen, and the house that I have built for your name, then hear from heaven your dwelling place their prayer and their pleas, maintain their cause and forgive your people who have sinned against you. (2 Chron 6:38-39, NRSVCE)
Hail Mary...

I will give them a heart, so that they may know me, that I am the Lord. And they will be my people, and I will be their God. For they shall return to me with their whole heart. (Jer 24:7)
Hail Mary...

You must change the way you are living and the things you are doing, and must obey the Lord your God. If you do, he will change his mind about the destruction that he said he would bring on you. (Jer 26:13, GNT)
Hail Mary...

Do not delay to turn back to the Lord, and do not postpone it from day to day. (Sir 5:7, NRSVCE)
Hail Mary...

Let us examine our ways, and seek out, and return to the Lord. Let us lift up our hearts, with our hands, toward the Lord in the heavens. (Lam 3:40-41)
Hail Mary...

I have taken off the garment of peace and have put on the sackcloth of supplication, and I will cry out to the most High in my days. (Bar 4:20)
Hail Mary...

Glory Be...

Decade 3

Our Father...

From the days of your fathers, you have withdrawn from my ordinances and have not kept them. Return to me, and I will return to you, says the Lord of hosts. (Mal 3:7)
Hail Mary...

Turn to me, says the Lord of hosts, and I will turn to you, says the Lord of hosts. (Zech 1:3)
Hail Mary...

In their tribulation, they will arise early to me. Come, let us return to the Lord. For he has seized us, and he will heal us. He will strike, and he will cure us. (Hos 6:1-2)
Hail Mary...

If you will return to me, and keep my precepts, and do them, even if you will have been led away to the furthest reaches of the heavens, I will gather you from there, and I will lead you back to the place that I have chosen so that my name would dwell there. (Neh 1:9)
Hail Mary...

In the past I knew only what others had told me, but now I have seen you with my own eyes. So I am ashamed of all I have said and repent in dust and ashes. (Job 42:5-6, GNT)
Hail Mary...

Just as you were once determined to turn away from God, now turn back and serve him with ten times more determination. (Bar 4:28, GNT)
Hail Mary...

Create in me a clean heart, O God, and put a new and right spirit within me. (Ps 51:10, NRSVCE)
Hail Mary...

Repent and be converted, so that your sins may be wiped away. And then, when the time of consolation will have arrived from the presence of the Lord, he will send the One who was foretold to you, Jesus Christ. (Acts 3:19-20)
Hail Mary...

Godly grief produces a repentance that leads to salvation and brings no regret, but worldly grief produces death. (2 Cor 7:10, NRSVCE)
Hail Mary...

Thus says the Lord God: Be converted, and withdraw from your idols, and turn your faces away from all your abominations. (Eze 14:6)
Hail Mary...

Glory Be...

Decade 4

Our Father...

If we confess our sins, then he is faithful and just, so as to forgive us our sins and to cleanse us from all iniquity. (1 Jn 1:9)
Hail Mary...

I acknowledged my sin to you, and I did not hide my iniquity; I said, "I will confess my transgressions to the Lord," and you forgave the guilt of my sin. (Ps 32:5, NRSVCE)
Hail Mary...

The Lord your God is kind and merciful, and if you return to him, he will accept you. (2 Chron 30:9, GNT)
Hail Mary...

The Lord will allow those who repent to return to him. He always gives encouragement to those who are losing hope. (Sir 17:24, GNT)
Hail Mary...

How great is the Lord's merciful forgiveness of those who turn to him! (Sir 17:29, GNT)
Hail Mary...

Have mercy on me, O God, according to your steadfast love; according to your abundant mercy blot out my transgressions. Wash me thoroughly from my iniquity, and cleanse me from my sin. (Ps 51:1-2, NRSVCE)
Hail Mary...

They will approach with weeping. And I will lead them back with mercy. And I will lead them through the torrents of water, by an upright way, and they will not stumble in it. (Jer 31:9)
Hail Mary...

Do you despise the riches of his goodness and patience and forbearance? Do you not know that the kindness of God is calling you to repentance? (Rom 2:4)
Hail Mary...

Remember, then, what you were taught and what you heard; obey it and turn from your sins. If you do not wake up, I will come upon you like a thief, and you will not even know the time when I will come. (Rev 3:3, GNT)
Hail Mary...

Call to mind the place from which you have fallen, and do penance, and do the first works. Otherwise, I will come to you and remove your lampstand from its place, unless you repent. (Rev 2:5)
Hail Mary...

Glory Be...

Decade 5

Our Father...

And God saw their works, that they had been converted from their evil way. And God took pity on them, concerning the harm that he had said he would do to them, and he did not do it. (Jon 3:10)
Hail Mary...

God, having looked down to see the ignorance of these times, has now announced to men that everyone everywhere should do penance. (Acts 17:30)
Hail Mary...

Those whom I love, I rebuke and chastise. Therefore, be zealous and do penance. Behold, I stand at the door and knock. If anyone will hear my voice and will open the door to me, I will enter to him, and I will dine with him, and he with me. (Rev 3:19-20)
Hail Mary...

Let the wicked leave their way of life and change their way of thinking. Let them turn to the Lord, our God; he is merciful and quick to forgive. (Is 55:7, GNT)
Hail Mary...

Come near to God, and he will come near to you. Wash your hands, you sinners! Purify your hearts, you hypocrites! Be sorrowful, cry, and weep; change your laughter into crying, your joy into gloom! Humble yourselves before the Lord, and he will lift you up. (Jas 4:8-10, GNT)
Hail Mary...

You shall be holy unto me, because I, the Lord, am holy, and I have separated you from the other peoples, so that you would be mine. (Lev 20:26)
Hail Mary...

If anyone, then, will have cleansed himself from these things, he shall be a vessel held in honor, sanctified and useful to the Lord, prepared for every good work. (2 Tim 2:21)
Hail Mary...

Let us cleanse ourselves from every defilement of body and of spirit, making holiness perfect in the fear of God. (2 Cor 7:1, NRSVCE)
Hail Mary...

I will cleanse them from all their iniquity, by which they have sinned against me. And I will forgive all their iniquities, by which they have offended against me and have despised me. (Jer 33:8)
Hail Mary...

I shall rise up and go to my father, and I will say to him: Father, I have sinned against heaven and before you. (Luk 15:18)
Hail Mary...

Glory Be...

Praise, Worship, & Thanksgiving

Decade 1

Our Father…

We give thanks to you, O God, we give thanks to you! We proclaim how great you are and tell of the wonderful things you have done. (Ps 75:1, GNT)
Hail Mary…

I will bless the Lord at all times; his praise shall continually be in my mouth. (Ps 34:1, NRSVCE)
Hail Mary…

Through him, let us offer the sacrifice of continual praise to God, which is the fruit of lips confessing his name. (Heb 13:15)
Hail Mary…

Let everything that breathes praise the Lord! (Ps 150:6, NRSVCE)
Hail Mary…

I call upon the Lord, who is worthy to be praised, and I am saved from my enemies. (2 Sam 22:4, NRSVCE)
Hail Mary…

You shall worship the Lord your God, and you shall serve him alone. (Luk 4:8)
Hail Mary…

O come, let us worship and bow down, let us kneel before the Lord, our Maker! For he is our God, and we are the people of his pasture, and the sheep of his hand. (Ps 95:6-7, NRSVCE)
Hail Mary…

Bless the Lord, O my soul, and all that is within me, bless his holy name. (Ps 103:1, NRSVCE)
Hail Mary…

From the rising of the sun to its setting the name of the Lord is to be praised. The Lord is high above all nations, and his glory above the heavens. (Ps 113:3-4, NRSVCE)
Hail Mary…

Come, bless the Lord, all you servants of the Lord, who stand by night in the house of the Lord! Lift up your hands to the holy place, and bless the Lord. (Ps 134:1-2, NRSVCE)
Hail Mary...

Glory Be...

Decade 2

Our Father...

Rejoice in the Lord, O you righteous. Praise befits the upright. (Ps 33:1, NRSVCE)
Hail Mary...

The Lord is my strength and my praise, and he has become my salvation. He is my God, and I shall glorify him. He is the God of my father, and I shall exalt him. (Exo 15:2)
Hail Mary...

For it was you who formed my inward parts; you knit me together in my mother's womb. I praise you, for I am fearfully and wonderfully made. Wonderful are your works. (Ps 139:13-14, NRSVCE)
Hail Mary...

Make a joyful noise to God, all the earth; sing the glory of his name; give to him glorious praise. (Ps 66:1-2, NRSVCE)
Hail Mary...

O Lord, open my lips, and my mouth will declare your praise. (Ps 51:15, NRSVCE)
Hail Mary...

 You are holy, enthroned on the praises of Israel. (Ps 22:3, NRSVCE)
Hail Mary...

To the King of ages, to the immortal, invisible, solitary God, be honor and glory forever and ever. Amen. (1 Tim 1:17)
Hail Mary

It is good to give thanks to the Lord, to sing praises to your name, O Most High; to declare your steadfast love in the morning, and your faithfulness by night. (Ps 92:1-2, NRSVCE)
Hail Mary

To the only God, our Savior, through Jesus Christ our Lord: to him be glory and magnificence, dominion and power, before all ages, and now, and in every age, forever. (Jude 1:25)
Hail Mary

The Lord is my strength and my shield; in him my heart trusts; so I am helped, and my heart exults, and with my song I give thanks to him. (Ps 28:7, NRSVCE)
Hail Mary

Glory Be…

Decade 3

Our Father…

Blessing and glory and wisdom and thanksgiving, honor and power and strength to our God, forever and ever. Amen. (Rev 7:12)
Hail Mary...

I will give thanks to the Lord with my whole heart, in the company of the upright, in the congregation. (Ps 111:1, NRSVCE)
Hail Mary...

Everything that God has created is good; nothing is to be rejected, but everything is to be received with a prayer of thanks, because the word of God and the prayer make it acceptable to God. (1 Tim 4:4-5, GNT)
Hail Mary...

Enter his gates with thanksgiving, and his courts with praise. Give thanks to him, bless his name. (Ps 100:4, NRSVCE)
Hail Mary...

I will thank you forever, because of what you have done. In the presence of the faithful I will proclaim your name, for it is good. (Ps 52:9, NRSVCE)
Hail Mary...

With my mouth I will give great thanks to the Lord; I will praise him in the midst of the throng. (Ps 109:30, NRSVCE)
Hail Mary...

Be anxious about nothing. But in all things, with prayer and supplication, with acts of thanksgiving, let your petitions be made known to God. (Phil 4:6)
Hail Mary...

O give thanks to the Lord, for he is good; for his steadfast love endures forever. (Ps 107:1, NRSVCE)
Hail Mary...

Praise the Lord! O give thanks to the Lord, for he is good; for his steadfast love endures forever. (Ps 106:1, NRSVCE)
Hail Mary...

Lifting up his eyes, Jesus said: "Father, I give thanks to you because you have heard me. And I know that you always hear me." (Jn 11:41)
Hail Mary...

Glory Be...

Decade 4

Our Father...

It was the duty of the trumpeters and singers to make themselves heard in unison in praise and thanksgiving to the Lord, and when the song was raised, with trumpets and cymbals and other musical instruments, in praise to the Lord, "For he is good, for his steadfast love endures forever," the house, the house of the Lord, was filled with a cloud. (2 Chron 5:13, NRSVCE)
Hail Mary...

Let us come into his presence with thanksgiving; let us make a joyful noise to him with songs of praise! For the Lord is a great God, and a great King above all gods. (Ps 95:2-3, NRSVCE)
Hail Mary...

Thank the Lord for his steadfast love, for his wonderful works to humankind. For he satisfies the thirsty, and the hungry he fills with good things. (Ps 107:8-9, NRSVCE)
Hail Mary...

Let everything whatsoever that you do, whether in word or in deed, be done all in the name of the Lord Jesus Christ, giving thanks to God the Father through him. (Col 3:17)

Hail Mary...

Let us be thankful, then, because we receive a kingdom that cannot be shaken. Let us be grateful and worship God in a way that will please him, with reverence and awe. (Heb 12:28, GNT)
Hail Mary...

Ascribe majesty to his name and give thanks to him with praise, with songs on your lips, and with harps. (Sir 39:15, NRSVCE)
Hail Mary...

Glorify the Lord and exalt him as much as you can, for he surpasses even that. When you exalt him, summon all your strength, and do not grow weary, for you cannot praise him enough. (Sir 43:30, NRSVCE)
Hail Mary...

I will always praise you and sing hymns of thanksgiving. You answered my prayer, and saved me from the threat of destruction. And so I thank you and praise you. O Lord, I praise you! (Sir 51:11, GNT)
Hail Mary...

You are the Lord our God, and we will praise you. You have made us fear you, so that we might pray to you. Here in exile we will praise you because we have turned away from the sins of our ancestors. (Bar 3:7, GNT)
Hail Mary...

Sing to God, sing praises to his name; lift up a song to him who rides upon the clouds—his name is the Lord—be exultant before him. (Ps 68:4, NRSVCE)
Hail Mary...

Glory Be...

Decade 5

Our Father...

Let the heavens rejoice, and let the earth exult. And let them say among the nations, 'The Lord has reigned.' (1 Chron 16:31)
Hail Mary...

Praise the Lord's glorious name; bring an offering and come into his Temple. Bow down before the Holy One when he appears; tremble before him, all the earth! (1 Chron 16:29-30, GNT)
Hail Mary...

The Lord is great in Zion; he is exalted over all the peoples. Let them praise your great and awesome name. Holy is he! (Ps 99:2-3, NRSVCE)
Hail Mary...

Praise him — he is your God, and you have seen with your own eyes the great and astounding things that he has done for you. (Deut 10:21, GNT)
Hail Mary...

I will tell of the Lord's unfailing love; I praise him for all he has done for us. He has richly blessed the people of Israel because of his mercy and constant love. (Is 63:7, GNT)
Hail Mary...

Not to us, O Lord, not to us, but to your name give glory, for the sake of your steadfast love and your faithfulness. (Ps 115:1, NRSVCE)
Hail Mary...

Lift up your heads, O gates! and be lifted up, O ancient doors! that the King of glory may come in. Who is the King of glory? The Lord, strong and mighty, the Lord, mighty in battle. (Ps 24:7-8, NRSVCE)
Hail Mary...

Give thanks in everything. For this is the will of God in Christ Jesus for all of you. (1 Thes 5:18)
Hail Mary...

Let not any kind of fornication, or impurity, so much as be named among you, just as is worthy of the saints, nor any indecent, or foolish, or abusive talk, for this is without purpose; but instead, give thanks. (Eph 5:3-4)
Hail Mary...

I will give to the Lord the thanks due to his righteousness, and sing praise to the name of the Lord, the Most High. (Ps 7:17, NRSVCE)
Hail Mary...

Glory Be...

The Eucharist

Decade 1

Our Father...

Do not work for food that perishes, but for that which endures to eternal life, which the Son of man will give to you. (Jn 6:27)
Hail Mary...

Therefore, Jesus said to them: "Amen, amen, I say to you, Moses did not give you bread from heaven, but my Father gives you the true bread from heaven." (Jn 6:32)
Hail Mary...

The bread of God is he who descends from heaven and gives life to the world. (Jn 6:33)
Hail Mary...

They said to him, "Lord, give us this bread always." (Jn 6:34)
Hail Mary...

Jesus said to them: "I am the bread of life. Whoever comes to me shall not hunger, and whoever believes in me shall never thirst." (Jn 6:35)
Hail Mary...

I am the bread of life. (Jn 6:48)
Hail Mary...

This is the bread which descends from heaven, so that if anyone will eat from it, he may not die. (Jn 6:50)
Hail Mary...

I am the living bread, who descended from heaven. (Jn 6:51)
Hail Mary...

If anyone eats from this bread, he shall live in eternity. And the bread that I will give is my flesh, for the life of the world. (Jn 6:52)
Hail Mary...

The Jews debated among themselves, saying, "How can this man give us his flesh to eat?" (Jn 6:53)
Hail Mary...

Glory Be…

Decade 2

Our Father…

Jesus said to them: "Amen, amen, I say to you, unless you eat the flesh of the Son of man and drink his blood, you will not have life in you." (Jn 6:54)
Hail Mary…

Whoever eats my flesh and drinks my blood has eternal life, and I will raise him up on the last day. (Jn 6:55)
Hail Mary…

My flesh is true food, and my blood is true drink. (Jn 6:56)
Hail Mary…

Whoever eats my flesh and drinks my blood abides in me, and I in him. (Jn 6:57)
Hail Mary…

Just as the living Father has sent me and I live because of the Father, so also whoever eats me, the same shall live because of me. (Jn 6:58)
Hail Mary…

The cup we use in the Lord's Supper and for which we give thanks to God: when we drink from it, we are sharing in the blood of Christ. And the bread we break: when we eat it, we are sharing in the body of Christ. (1 Cor 10:16, GNT)
Hail Mary…

Through the one bread, we, though many, are one body: all of us who are partakers of the one bread. (1 Cor 10:17)
Hail Mary…

He gave them grain from heaven, by sending down manna for them to eat. So they ate the food of angels, and God gave them all they wanted. (Ps 78:24-25, GNT)
Hail Mary…

I have received from the Lord what I have also delivered to you: that the Lord Jesus, on the same night that he was handed over, took bread, and giving thanks, he broke it, and said: "Take and eat. This is

my body, which shall be given up for you. Do this in remembrance of me." (1 Cor 11:23-24)
Hail Mary...

Similarly also, the cup, after he had eaten supper, saying: "This cup is the new covenant in my blood. Do this, as often as you drink it, in remembrance of me." (1 Cor 11:25)
Hail Mary...

Glory Be...

Decade 3

Our Father...

For as often as you eat this bread and drink the cup, you proclaim the Lord's death until he comes. (1 Cor 11:26, NRSVCE)
Hail Mary...

Whoever eats this bread, or drinks from the cup of the Lord, unworthily, shall be liable of the body and blood of the Lord. (1 Cor 11:27)
Hail Mary...

Examine yourselves, and only then eat of the bread and drink of the cup. (1 Cor 11:28, NRSVCE)
Hail Mary...

Whoever eats and drinks unworthily, eats and drinks a sentence against himself, not discerning it to be the body of the Lord. (1 Cor 11:29)
Hail Mary...

You are the temple of the living God, just as God says: "I will dwell with them, and I will walk among them. And I will be their God, and they shall be my people." (2 Cor 6:16)
Hail Mary...

He sat down to eat with them, took the bread, and said the blessing; then he broke the bread and gave it to them. Then their eyes were opened and they recognized him, but he disappeared from their sight. (Luk 24:30-31, GNT)
Hail Mary...

They devoted themselves to the apostles' teaching and fellowship, to the breaking of bread and the prayers. (Acts 2:42, NRSVCE)
Hail Mary...

Day after day they met as a group in the Temple, and they had their meals together in their homes, eating with glad and humble hearts, praising God, and enjoying the good will of all the people. And every day the Lord added to their group those who were being saved. (Acts 2:46-47, GNT)
Hail Mary...

When the hour had arrived, he sat down at table, and the twelve Apostles with him. And he said to them: "With longing have I desired to eat this Passover with you, before I suffer." (Luk 22:14-15)
Hail Mary...

I say to you, that from this time, I will not eat it, until it is fulfilled in the Kingdom of God. (Luk 22:16)
Hail Mary...

Glory Be...

Decade 4

Our Father...

Having taken the chalice, he gave thanks, and he said: "Take this and share it among yourselves." (Luk 22:17)
Hail Mary...

I say to you, that I will not drink from the fruit of the vine, until the Kingdom of God arrives. (Luk 22:18)
Hail Mary...

He took a piece of bread, gave thanks to God, broke it, and gave it to them, saying, "This is my body, which is given for you. Do this in memory of me." (Luk 22:19, GNT)
Hail Mary...

In the same way, he gave them the cup after the supper, saying, "This cup is God's new covenant sealed with my blood, which is poured out for you." (Luk 22:20, GNT)
Hail Mary...

The two then explained to them what had happened on the road, and how they had recognized the Lord when he broke the bread. (Luk 24:35, GNT)
Hail Mary...

On the first day of the week, when we met to break bread, Paul was holding a discussion with them; since he intended to leave the next day, he continued speaking until midnight. (Acts 20:7, NRSVCE)
Hail Mary...

He ordered the crowd to sit down on the ground. Then he took the seven loaves, gave thanks to God, broke them, and gave them to his disciples to distribute to the crowd; and the disciples did so. (Mrk 8:6, GNT)
Hail Mary...

Melchizedek, the king of Salem, brought forth bread and wine, for he was a priest of the Most High God; he blessed him, and he said: "Blessed be Abram by the Most High God, who created heaven and earth. And blessed be the Most High God, through whose protection the enemies are in your hands." And he gave him tithes from everything. (Gen 14:18-20)
Hail Mary...

Your lamb shall be without blemish, a year-old male; you may take it from the sheep or from the goats. You shall keep it until the fourteenth day of this month; then the whole assembled congregation of Israel shall slaughter it at twilight. (Exo 12:5-6, NRSVCE)
Hail Mary...

On the next day, John saw Jesus coming toward him, and so he said: "Behold, the Lamb of God. Behold, he who takes away the sin of the world." (Jn 1:29)
Hail Mary...

Glory Be...

Decade 5

Our Father...

The centurion said: "Lord, I am not worthy that you should enter under my roof, but only say the word, and my servant shall be healed." (Matt 8:8)

Hail Mary...

The angel said to me, "Write this: Happy are those who have been invited to the wedding feast of the Lamb." And the angel added, "These are the true words of God." (Rev 19:9, GNT)
Hail Mary...

I saw, and behold, in the midst of the throne and the four living creatures, and in the midst of the elders, a Lamb was standing, as if it were slain, having seven horns and seven eyes, which are the seven spirits of God, sent forth to all the earth. (Rev 5:6)
Hail Mary...

They sang a new song: You are worthy to take the scroll and to break open its seals. For you were killed, and by your sacrificial death you bought for God people from every tribe, language, nation, and race. (Rev 5:9, GNT)
Hail Mary...

The crowds that preceded him, and those that followed, cried out, saying: "Hosanna to the Son of David! Blessed is he who comes in the name of the Lord. Hosanna in the highest!" (Matt 21:9)
Hail Mary...

Let us rejoice and be glad; let us praise his greatness! For the time has come for the wedding of the Lamb, and his bride has prepared herself for it. (Rev 19:7, GNT)
Hail Mary...

While eating with them, Jesus took bread. And blessing it, he broke it and gave it to them, and he said: "Take. This is my body." (Mrk 14:22)
Hail Mary...

Having taken the chalice, giving thanks, he gave it to them. And they all drank from it. And he said to them: "This is my blood of the new covenant, which shall be shed for many." (Mrk 14:23-24)
Hail Mary...

Amen I say to you, that I will no longer drink from this fruit of the vine, until that day when I will drink it new in the Kingdom of God. (Mrk 14:25)
Hail Mary...

You nourished your people with the food of angels, and, having prepared bread from heaven, you served them without labor that which holds within itself every delight and the sweetness of every flavor. (Wis 16:20)
Hail Mary...

Glory Be...

Ministry and Evangelization

Decade 1

Our Father...

I will give you such words and wisdom that none of your enemies will be able to refute or contradict what you say. (Luk 21:15, GNT)
Hail Mary...

Give to me wisdom and understanding, so that I may enter and depart before your people. For who is able worthily to judge this, your people, who are so great? (2 Chron 1:10)
Hail Mary...

With great power, the Apostles were rendering testimony to the Resurrection of Jesus Christ our Lord. And great grace was in them all. (Acts 4:33)
Hail Mary...

Do your best to win full approval in God's sight, as a worker who is not ashamed of his work, one who correctly teaches the message of God's truth. (2 Tim 2:15, GNT)
Hail Mary...

You will tell them whatever I tell you to say, whether they listen or not. (Eze 2:7, GNT)
Hail Mary...

Do not be afraid. Instead, speak out and do not be silent. For I am with you. And no one will take hold of you, so as to do you harm. (Acts 18:9-10)
Hail Mary...

You shall go forth to everyone to whom I will send you. And you shall speak all that I will command you." (Jer 1:7)
Hail Mary...

Today I have appointed you over nations and over kingdoms, so that you may root up, and pull down, and destroy, and scatter, and so that you may build and plant. (Jer 1:10)
Hail Mary...

Go and tell them everything I command you to say. Do not be afraid of them. (Jer 1:17, GNT)
Hail Mary…

While Peter was still speaking these words, the Holy Spirit fell over all of those who were listening to the Word. (Acts 10:44)
Hail Mary…

Glory Be…

Decade 2

Our Father…

I have made you a tester and a refiner among my people so that you may know and test their ways. (Jer 6:27, NRSVCE)
Hail Mary…

Amen, amen, I say to you, whoever believes in me shall also do the works that I do. And greater things than these shall he do, for I go to the Father. (Jn 14:12)
Hail Mary…

I myself will prepare your way, leveling mountains and hills. I will break down bronze gates and smash their iron bars. I will give you treasures from dark, secret places; then you will know that I am the Lord and that the God of Israel has called you by name. (Is 45:2-3, GNT)
Hail Mary…

The Spirit of the Lord has spoken through me, and his word was spoken through my tongue. (2 Sam 23:2)
Hail Mary…

I have established you like a new threshing cart, having serrated blades. You will thresh the mountains and crush them. And you will turn the hills into chaff. (Is 41:15)
Hail Mary…

You are my war club, my weapon of battle: with you I smash nations; with you I destroy kingdoms; with you I smash the horse and its rider; with you I smash the chariot and the charioteer. (Jer 51:20-21)
Hail Mary…

Do not fear them. For nothing is covered that shall not be revealed, nor hidden that shall not be known. What I tell you in darkness, speak in the light. And what you hear whispered in the ear, preach above the rooftops. (Matt 10:26-27)
Hail Mary...

Go on, therefore, and I will be in your mouth. And I will teach you what you shall say. (Exo 4:12)
Hail Mary...

My sons, do not choose to be negligent. The Lord has chosen you so that you would stand before him, and minister to him, and worship him. (2 Chron 29:11)
Hail Mary...

My words and preaching were not the persuasive words of human wisdom, but were a manifestation of the Spirit and of virtue, so that your faith would not be based on the wisdom of men, but on the virtue of God. (1 Cor 2:4-5)
Hail Mary...

Glory Be...

Decade 3

Our Father...

Places that have been desolate for ages will be built up by you. You will raise a foundation for generation after generation. And you will be called the repairer of hedges, who turns the roadways into quiet places. (Is 58:12)
Hail Mary...

Cry out! Cease not! Exalt your voice like a trumpet, and announce to my people their wicked acts, and to the house of Jacob their sins. (Is 58:1)
Hail Mary...

You are a chosen race, a royal priesthood, a holy nation, God's own people, in order that you may proclaim the mighty acts of him who called you out of darkness into his marvelous light. (1 Pet 2:9, NRSVCE)
Hail Mary...

Sanctify Christ the Lord in your hearts, being always ready to give an explanation to all who ask you the reason for that hope which is in you. (1 Pet 3:15)
Hail Mary…

Each one, as a good manager of God's different gifts, must use for the good of others the special gift he has received from God. Those who preach must preach God's messages; those who serve must serve with the strength that God gives them, so that in all things praise may be given to God through Jesus Christ, to whom belong glory and power forever and ever. (1 Pet 4:10-11, GNT)
Hail Mary…

He said to them: "Go forth to the whole world and preach the Gospel to every creature." (Mrk 16:15)
Hail Mary…

We preach Christ to everyone. With all possible wisdom we warn and teach them in order to bring each one into God's presence as a mature individual in union with Christ.To get this done I toil and struggle, using the mighty strength which Christ supplies and which is at work in me. (Col 1:28-29, GNT)
Hail Mary…

I give thanks to Christ Jesus our Lord, who has given me strength for my work. I thank him for considering me worthy and appointing me to serve him. (1 Tim 1:12, GNT)
Hail Mary…

O give thanks to the Lord, call on his name, make known his deeds among the peoples. (Ps 105:1, NRSVCE)
Hail Mary…

Use your full authority as you encourage and rebuke your hearers. Let none of them look down on you. (Tit 2:15, GNT)
Hail Mary…

Glory Be…

Decade 4

Our Father…

Sing to the Lord, bless his name; tell of his salvation from day to day. Declare his glory among the nations, his marvelous works among all the peoples. (Ps 96:2-3, NRSVCE)
Hail Mary...

My dear friends, stand firm and steady. Keep busy always in your work for the Lord, since you know that nothing you do in the Lord's service is ever useless. (1 Cor 15:58, GNT)
Hail Mary...

These have the power to close up the heavens, so that it may not rain during the days of their prophesying. And they have power over the waters, to convert them into blood, and to strike the earth with every kind of affliction as often as they will. (Rev 11:6)
Hail Mary...

I will not enter my house or get into my bed; I will not give sleep to my eyes or slumber to my eyelids, until I find a place for the Lord, a dwelling place for the Mighty One of Jacob. (Ps 132:3-5, NRSVCE)
Hail Mary...

The Lord has called me from the womb; from the womb of my mother, he has been mindful of my name. And he has appointed my mouth as a sharp sword. In the shadow of his hand, he has protected me. And he has appointed me as an elect arrow. In his quiver, he has hidden me. (Is 49:1-2)
Hail Mary...

The Lord said to me, "I have a greater task for you, my servant. Not only will you restore to greatness the people of Israel who have survived, but I will also make you a light to the nations—so that all the world may be saved." (Is 49:6, GNT)
Hail Mary...

The kings will see, and the princes will rise up, and they will adore, because of the Lord. For he is faithful, and he is the Holy One of Israel, who has chosen you. (Is 49:7)
Hail Mary...

I have told the glad news of deliverance in the great congregation; see, I have not restrained my lips, as you know, O Lord. (Ps 40:9, NRSVCE)
Hail Mary...

If you turn back, I will take you back, and you shall stand before me. If you utter what is precious, and not what is worthless, you shall serve as my mouth. It is they who will turn to you, not you who will turn to them. (Jer 15:19, NRSVCE)
Hail Mary...

You shall speak all that I command you. (Exo 7:2, NRSVCE)
Hail Mary...

Glory Be...

Decade 5

Our Father...

I will sing of your steadfast love, O Lord, forever; with my mouth I will proclaim your faithfulness to all generations. (Ps 89:1, NRSVCE)
Hail Mary...

My child, if you are going to serve the Lord, be prepared for times when you will be put to the test. Be sincere and determined. Keep calm when trouble comes. (Sir 2:1-2, GNT)
Hail Mary...

And now, Lord, take notice of the threats they have made, and allow us, your servants, to speak your message with all boldness. Reach out your hand to heal, and grant that wonders and miracles may be performed through the name of your holy Servant Jesus. (Acts 4:29-30, GNT)
Hail Mary...

He called the twelve. And he began to send them out in twos, and he gave them authority over unclean spirits. (Mrk 6:7)
Hail Mary...

Truly I have been filled with the strength of the Spirit of the Lord, with judgment and virtue, in order to announce to Jacob his wickedness and to Israel his sin. (Mic 3:8)
Hail Mary...

Open your works to the Lord, and your intentions will be set in order. (Pro 16:3)
Hail Mary...

God chose what is foolish in the world to shame the wise; God chose what is weak in the world to shame the strong; God chose what is low and despised in the world, things that are not, to reduce to nothing things that are, so that no one might boast in the presence of God. (1 Cor 1:27-29, NRSVCE)
Hail Mary…

Choose today what pleases you, and whom you ought to serve above all else: but as for me and my house, we will serve the Lord. (Josh 24:15)
Hail Mary…

Brothers and sisters, be all the more eager to confirm your call and election, for if you do this, you will never stumble. (2 Pet 1:10, NRSVCE)
Hail Mary…

But as for you, truly, be vigilant, laboring in all things. Do the work of an Evangelist, fulfilling your ministry. Show self-restraint. (2 Tim 4:5)
Hail Mary…

Glory Be…

Suffering/ Hope/ Patience

Decade 1

Our Father...

They strengthened the souls of the disciples and encouraged them to continue in the faith, saying, "It is through many persecutions that we must enter the kingdom of God." (Acts 14:22, NRSVCE)
Hail Mary...

Suffering produces endurance, and endurance produces character, and character produces hope. (Rom 5:3-4, NRSVCE)
Hail Mary...

I consider that the sufferings of this time are not worthy to be compared with that future glory which shall be revealed in us. (Rom 8:18)
Hail Mary...

I will exult and rejoice in your steadfast love, because you have seen my affliction; you have taken heed of my adversities. (Ps 31:7, NRSVCE)
Hail Mary...

We do not lose heart. Even though our outer nature is wasting away, our inner nature is being renewed day by day. (2 Cor 4:16, NRSVCE)
Hail Mary...

This small and temporary trouble we suffer will bring us a tremendous and eternal glory, much greater than the trouble. For we fix our attention, not on things that are seen, but on things that are unseen. What can be seen lasts only for a time, but what cannot be seen lasts forever. (2 Cor 4:17-18, GNT)
Hail Mary...

I am now rejoicing in my sufferings for your sake, and in my flesh I am completing what is lacking in Christ's afflictions for the sake of his body, that is, the church. (Col 1:24, NRSVCE)
Hail Mary...

My friends, consider yourselves fortunate when all kinds of trials come your way, for you know that when your faith succeeds in facing such trials, the result is the ability to endure. (Jas 1:2-3, GNT)
Hail Mary...

We are afflicted in every way, but not crushed; perplexed, but not driven to despair; persecuted, but not forsaken; struck down, but not destroyed; always carrying in the body the death of Jesus, so that the life of Jesus may also be made visible in our bodies. (2 Cor 4:8-10, NRSVCE)
Hail Mary...

We know that in all things God works for good with those who love him, those whom he has called according to his purpose. (Rom 8:28, GNT)
Hail Mary...

Glory Be...

Decade 2

Our Father...

If you suffer because you are a Christian, don't be ashamed of it, but thank God that you bear Christ's name. (1 Pet 4:16, GNT)
Hail Mary...

Happy are you if you are insulted because you are Christ's followers; this means that the glorious Spirit, the Spirit of God, is resting on you. (1 Pet 4:14, GNT)
Hail Mary...

I am content with weaknesses, insults, hardships, persecutions, and difficulties for Christ's sake. For when I am weak, then I am strong. (2 Cor 12:10, GNT)
Hail Mary...

The God of all grace, who has called us to his eternal glory in Christ Jesus, will himself perfect, confirm, and establish us, after a brief time of suffering. (1 Pet 5:10)
Hail Mary...

Be glad about this, even though it may now be necessary for you to be sad for a while because of the many kinds of trials you suffer. Their

purpose is to prove that your faith is genuine. Even gold, which can be destroyed, is tested by fire; and so your faith, which is much more precious than gold, must also be tested, so that it may endure. Then you will receive praise and glory and honor on the Day when Jesus Christ is revealed. (1 Pet 1:6-7)
Hail Mary…

For it is a credit to you if, being aware of God, you endure pain while suffering unjustly. (1 Pet 2:19, NRSVCE)
Hail Mary…

It was to this that God called you, for Christ himself suffered for you and left you an example, so that you would follow in his steps. (1 Pet 2:21, GNT)
Hail Mary…

When he was insulted, he did not answer back with an insult; when he suffered, he did not threaten, but placed his hopes in God, the righteous Judge. (1 Pet 2:23, GNT)
Hail Mary…

My friends, remember the prophets who spoke in the name of the Lord. Take them as examples of patient endurance under suffering. We call them happy because they endured. You have heard of Job's patience, and you know how the Lord provided for him in the end. For the Lord is full of mercy and compassion. (Jas 5:10-11, GNT)
Hail Mary…

Are any among you in trouble? They should pray. Are any among you happy? They should sing praises. (Jas 5:13, GNT)
Hail Mary…

Glory Be…

Decade 3

Our Father…

In me you may have peace. In the world you face persecution. But take courage; I have conquered the world! (Jn 16:33, NRSVCE)
Hail Mary…

God will wipe away every tear from their eyes. And death shall be no more. And neither mourning, nor crying out, nor grief shall be anymore. For the first things have passed away. (Rev 21:4)
Hail Mary…

Why are you cast down, O my soul, and why are you disquieted within me? Hope in God; for I shall again praise him, my help and my God. (Ps 42:11, NRSVCE)
Hail Mary…

Blessed be the God and Father of our Lord Jesus Christ, the Father of mercies and the God of all consolation. He consoles us in all our tribulation, so that we too may be able to console those who are in any kind of distress, through the exhortation by which we also are being exhorted by God. (2 Cor 1:3-4)
Hail Mary…

He who rescued us from so deadly a peril will continue to rescue us; on him we have set our hope that he will rescue us again. (2 Cor 1:10, NRSVCE)
Hail Mary…

Cast all your anxiety on him, because he cares for you. (1 Pet 5:7, NRSVCE)
Hail Mary…

No testing has overtaken you that is not common to everyone. God is faithful, and he will not let you be tested beyond your strength, but with the testing he will also provide the way out so that you may be able to endure it. (1 Cor 10:13, NRSVCE)
Hail Mary…

Do not be afraid, for I am with you. Do not turn away, for I am your God. I have strengthened you, and I have assisted you, and the right hand of my just one has upheld you. (Is 41:10)
Hail Mary…

You have kept count of my tossings; put my tears in your bottle. Are they not in your record? (Ps 56:8, NRSVCE)
Hail Mary…

This poor soul cried, and was heard by the Lord, and was saved from every trouble. (Ps 34:6, NRSVCE)
Hail Mary…

Glory Be...

Decade 4

Our Father...

The eyes of the Lord are on the righteous, and his ears are open to their cry. (Ps 34:15, NRSVCE)
Hail Mary...

When the righteous cry for help, the Lord hears, and rescues them from all their troubles. (Ps 34:17, NRSVCE)
Hail Mary...

The Lord is near to the brokenhearted, and saves the crushed in spirit. (Ps 34:18, NRSVCE)
Hail Mary...

Many are the afflictions of the righteous, but the Lord rescues them from them all. (Ps 34:19, NRSVCE)
Hail Mary...

His anger is but for a moment; his favor is for a lifetime. Weeping may linger for the night, but joy comes with the morning. (Ps 30:5, NRSVCE)
Hail Mary...

You have turned my mourning into dancing; you have taken off my sackcloth and clothed me with joy. (Ps 30:11, NRSVCE)
Hail Mary...

I lift up my eyes to the hills—from where will my help come? My help comes from the Lord, who made heaven and earth. (Ps 121:1-2, NRSVCE)
Hail Mary...

He will hide me in his shelter in the day of trouble; he will conceal me under the cover of his tent; he will set me high on a rock. (Ps 27:5, NRSVCE)
Hail Mary...

Call on me in the day of trouble; I will deliver you, and you shall glorify me. (Ps 50:15, NRSVCE)
Hail Mary...

Peace I leave for you; my Peace I give to you. Not in the way that the world gives, do I give to you. Do not let your heart be troubled, and let it not fear. (Jn 14:27)
Hail Mary…

Glory Be…

Decade 5

Our Father…

Take off, O Jerusalem, the garment of your sorrow and troubles, and put on your beauty and the honor of that eternal glory, which you have from God. (Bar 5:1)
Hail Mary…

The needy shall not always be forgotten, nor the hope of the poor perish forever. (Ps 9:18, NRSVCE)
Hail Mary…

Happy are those whose help is the God of Jacob, whose hope is in the Lord their God. (Ps 146:5, NRSVCE)
Hail Mary…

Behold, I am instructing you. Be strengthened, and be steadfast. Do not dread, and do not fear. For the Lord your God is with you in all things, wherever you may go. (Josh 1:9)
Hail Mary…

Be strengthened and be very steadfast, so that you may observe and accomplish the entire law. You may not turn aside from it to the right, nor to the left. So may you understand all that you should do. (Josh 1:7)
Hail Mary…

You have been given the privilege of serving Christ, not only by believing in him, but also by suffering for him. (Phil 1:29, GNT)
Hail Mary…

It was by hope that we were saved; but if we see what we hope for, then it is not really hope. For who of us hopes for something we see? But if we hope for what we do not see, we wait for it with patience. (Rom 8:24-25, GNT)
Hail Mary…

Blessed are they that suffer persecution for justice' sake: for theirs is the kingdom of heaven. Blessed are you when they shall revile you, and persecute you, and speak all that is evil against you, untruly, for my sake: Be glad and rejoice, for your reward is very great in heaven. (Matt 5:10-12, DRA)
Hail Mary…

What credit is there if you endure the beatings you deserve for having done wrong? But if you endure suffering even when you have done right, God will bless you for it. (1 Pet 2:20, GNT)
Hail Mary…

For it is better to suffer for doing good, if it is the will of God, than for doing evil. (1 Pet 3:17)
Hail Mary…

Glory Be…

Sin

Decade 1

Our Father…

In your struggle against sin you have not yet resisted to the point of shedding your blood. (Heb 12:4, NRSVCE)
Hail Mary…

Jesus answered them: "Amen, amen, I say to you, that everyone who commits sin is a slave of sin." (Jn 8:34)
Hail Mary…

If we claim that we have no sin, then we are deceiving ourselves and the truth is not in us. (1 Jn 1:8)
Hail Mary…

If we do not do the good we know we should do, we are guilty of sin. (Jas 4:17, NRSVCE)
Hail Mary…

The wages of sin is death. But the free gift of God is eternal life in Christ Jesus our Lord. (Rom 6:23)
Hail Mary…

Since all have sinned and fall short of the glory of God; they are now justified by his grace as a gift, through the redemption that is in Christ Jesus, whom God put forward as a sacrifice of atonement by his blood, effective through faith. (Rom 3:23-25, NRSVCE)
Hail Mary…

Therefore, just as through one man sin entered into this world, and through sin, death; so also death was transferred to all men, to all who have sinned. (Rom 5:12)
Hail Mary…

Whoever continues to sin belongs to the Devil, because the Devil has sinned from the very beginning. The Son of God appeared for this very reason, to destroy what the Devil had done. (1 Jn 3:8, NRSVCE)
Hail Mary…

Whoever sins is guilty of breaking God's law, because sin is a breaking of the law. (1 Jn 3:4, GNT)
Hail Mary...

Those who are children of God do not continue to sin, for God's very nature is in them; and because God is their Father, they cannot continue to sin. (1 Jn 3:9, GNT)
Hail Mary...

Glory Be...

Decade 2

Our Father...

No one, when tempted, should say, "I am being tempted by God"; for God cannot be tempted by evil and he himself tempts no one. (Jas 1:13, NRSVCE)
Hail Mary...

We are tempted when we are drawn away and trapped by our own evil desires. Then our evil desires conceive and give birth to sin; and sin, when it is full-grown, gives birth to death. (Jas 1:14-15, GNT)
Hail Mary...

If your hand or your foot leads you to sin, cut it off and cast it away from you. It is better for you to enter into life disabled or lame, than to be sent into eternal fire having two hands or two feet. (Matt 18:8)
Hail Mary...

In as much as he himself has suffered and has been tempted, he also is able to assist those who are tempted. (Heb 2:18)
Hail Mary...

Since Christ suffered physically, you too must strengthen yourselves with the same way of thinking that he had; because whoever suffers physically is no longer involved with sin. From now on, then, you must live the rest of your earthly lives controlled by God's will and not by human desires. (1 Pet 4:1-2, GNT)
Hail Mary...

Blessed is the man who suffers temptation. For when he has been proven, he shall receive the crown of life which God has promised to those who love him. (Jas 1:12)

Hail Mary…

He said to me, "My grace is sufficient for you, for power is made perfect in weakness." So, I will boast all the more gladly of my weaknesses, so that the power of Christ may dwell in me. (2 Cor 12:9, NRSVCE)
Hail Mary…

Keep my steps steady according to your promise, and never let iniquity have dominion over me. (Ps 119:133, NRSVCE)
Hail Mary…

Let us have confidence, then, and approach God's throne, where there is grace. There we will receive mercy and find grace to help us just when we need it. (Heb 4:16, GNT)
Hail Mary…

Come now, let us argue it out, says the Lord: though your sins are like scarlet, they shall be like snow; though they are red like crimson, they shall become like wool. (Is 1:18, NRSVCE)
Hail Mary…

Glory Be…

Decade 3

Our Father…

I will carry the wrath of the Lord, because I have sinned against him, until he may judge my case and execute judgment for me. He will lead me into the light. I will behold his justice. (Mic 7:9)
Hail Mary…

I will forgive their iniquities, and I will no longer remember their sins. (Heb 8:12)
Hail Mary…

He will turn back and have mercy on us. He will put away our iniquities, and he will cast all our sins into the depths of the sea. (Mic 7:19)
Hail Mary…

Our former selves have been crucified together with him, so that the body which is of sin may be destroyed, and moreover, so that we may

no longer serve sin. For he who has died has been justified from sin. (Rom 6:6-7)
Hail Mary…

You must put to death, then, the earthly desires at work in you, such as sexual immorality, indecency, lust, evil passions, and greed. Because of such things God's anger will come upon those who do not obey him. (Col 3:5-6, GNT)
Hail Mary…

From the inside, from your heart, come the evil ideas which lead you to do immoral things, to rob, kill, commit adultery, be greedy, and do all sorts of evil things; deceit, indecency, jealousy, slander, pride, and folly—all these evil things come from inside you and make you unclean. (Mrk 7:21-23, GNT)
Hail Mary…

If you do well, will you not be accepted? And if you do not do well, sin is lurking at the door; its desire is for you, but you must master it. (Gen 4:7, NRSVCE)
Hail Mary…

Be obedient to God, and do not allow your lives to be shaped by those desires you had when you were still ignorant. Instead, be holy in all that you do, just as God who called you is holy. (1 Pet 1:14-15, GNT)
Hail Mary…

You have heard that it was said, 'Do not commit adultery.' But now I tell you: anyone who looks at a woman and wants to possess her is guilty of committing adultery with her in his heart. (Matt 5:27-28, GNT)
Hail Mary…

We know that those who are born of God do not sin, but the one who was born of God protects them, and the evil one does not touch them. (1 Jn 5:18, NRSVCE)
Hail Mary…

Glory Be…

Decade 4

Our Father…

Behold, the hand of the Lord has not been shortened, so that it cannot save, and his ear has not been blocked, so that it cannot hear. But your iniquities have made a division between you and your God, and your sins have concealed his face from you, so that he would not hear. (Is 59:1-2)
Hail Mary…

No one who conceals transgressions will prosper, but one who confesses and forsakes them will obtain mercy. (Pro 28:13, NRSVCE)
Hail Mary…

A man who fasts for his sins, and then does the same again, what was the benefit of his humbling himself? Who will heed his prayer? (Sir 34:31)
Hail Mary…

If we walk in the light, just as he also is in the light, then we have fellowship with one another, and the blood of Jesus Christ, his Son, cleanses us from all sin. (1 Jn 1:7)
Hail Mary…

I am writing this to you, my children, so that you will not sin; but if anyone does sin, we have someone who pleads with the Father on our behalf — Jesus Christ, the righteous one. (1 Jn 2:1, GNT)
Hail Mary…

"All things are lawful for me," but not all things are beneficial. "All things are lawful for me," but I will not be dominated by anything. (1 Cor 6:12, NRSVCE)
Hail Mary…

Jesus found him in the Temple and said, "Listen, you are well now; so stop sinning or something worse may happen to you." (Jn 5:14, GNT)
Hail Mary…

Those who fear the Lord do not disobey his commands; those who love him will live as he wants them to live. Those who fear and love the Lord will try to please him and devote themselves to the Law. (Sir 2:15-16, GNT)
Hail Mary…

I will form an everlasting covenant with them, and I will not cease to do good for them. And I will put my fear into their heart, so that they do not withdraw from me. (Jer 32:40)
Hail Mary…

Sin shall not have dominion over you; for you are not under the law, but under grace. (Rom 6:14, DRA)
Hail Mary…

Glory Be…

Decade 5

Our Father…

Whatever you do, remember that some day you must die. As long as you keep this in mind, you will never sin. (Sir 7:36, GNT)
Hail Mary…

Do not say, "I sinned, yet what has happened to me?" for the Lord is slow to anger. Do not be so confident of forgiveness that you add sin to sin. (Sir 5:4-5, NRSVCE)
Hail Mary…

If you are wise, you will be careful in everything you do. When sin is all around you, be especially careful that you do not become guilty. (Sir 18:27, GNT)
Hail Mary…

My child, have you sinned? Don't do it again, and pray for forgiveness for what you have already done. (Sir 21:1, GNT)
Hail Mary…

Flee from sins, as if from the face of a serpent. For if you approach them, they will take hold of you. (Sir 21:2)
Hail Mary…

The synagogue of sinners is like stubble piled up; for the end of them both is a burning fire. (Sir 21:10)
Hail Mary…

In him, we have redemption through his blood: the remission of sins in accord with the riches of his grace. (Eph 1:7)
Hail Mary…

He has never commanded anyone to be wicked or given anyone permission to sin. (Sir 15:20, GNT)
Hail Mary...

Be vigilant and pray, so that you may not enter into temptation. Indeed, the spirit is willing, but the flesh is weak. (Matt 26:41)
Hail Mary...

God's divine power has given us everything we need to live a truly religious life through our knowledge of the one who called us to share in his own glory and goodness. (2 Pet 1:3, GNT)
Hail Mary...

Glory Be...

Prayer and Faith

Decade 1

Our Father…

Serve the Lord willingly, and the Lord will accept you; your prayers will reach the skies. (Sir 35:16, GNT)
Hail Mary…

You have humbled yourself before me, and have rent your clothes and wept before me, I also have heard you, says the Lord. (2 Chron 34:27, RSVCE)
Hail Mary…

When you call upon me and come and pray to me, I will hear you. When you search for me, you will find me; if you seek me with all your heart, I will let you find me, says the Lord. (Jer 29:12-14, NRSVCE)
Hail Mary…

I will rescue those who love me. I will protect those who trust in my name. When they call on me, I will answer; I will be with them in trouble. I will rescue and honor them. (Ps 91:14-15, NLT)
Hail Mary…

Listen closely to my prayer, O Lord; hear my urgent cry. I will call to you whenever I'm in trouble, and you will answer me. (Ps 86:6-7, NLT)
Hail Mary…

If you abide in me, and my words abide in you, then you may ask for whatever you will, and it shall be done for you. (Jn 15:7)
Hail Mary…

While he was in distress he entreated the favor of the Lord his God and humbled himself greatly before the God of his ancestors. He prayed to him, and God received his entreaty, heard his plea, and restored him. (2 Chron 33:12-13, NRSVCE)
Hail Mary…

Before they call I will answer, while they are yet speaking I will hear. (Is 65:24, NRSVCE)
Hail Mary...

Whatever you ask for in prayer, believe that you have received it, and it will be yours. (Mrk 11:24, NRSVCE)
Hail Mary...

Every child of God is able to defeat the world. And we win the victory over the world by means of our faith. (1 Jn 5:4, GNT)
Hail Mary...

Glory Be...

Decade 2

Our Father...

You, when you pray, enter into your room, and having shut the door, pray to your Father in secret, and your Father, who sees in secret, will repay you. (Matt 6:6)
Hail Mary...

When you are praying, do not heap up empty phrases as the Gentiles do; for they think that they will be heard because of their many words. Do not be like them, for your Father knows what you need before you ask him. (Matt 6:7-8, NRSVCE)
Hail Mary...

The prayer of the righteous is powerful and effective. (Jas 5:16, NRSVCE)
Hail Mary...

Call to me and I will answer you, and will tell you great and hidden things which you have not known. (Jer 33:3, RSVCE)
Hail Mary...

The eyes of the Lord are upon the just, and his ears are with their prayers. (1 Pet 3:12)
Hail Mary...

Be persistent in prayer, and keep alert as you pray, giving thanks to God. (Col 4:2, GNT)
Hail Mary...

All things can be done for the one who believes. (Mrk 9:23)

Hail Mary...

We walk by faith, not by sight. (2 Cor 5:7, NRSVCE)
Hail Mary...

Now to him who by the power at work within us is able to accomplish abundantly far more than all we can ask or imagine. (Eph 3:20, NRSVCE)
Hail Mary...

Ask in faith, never doubting, for the one who doubts is like a wave of the sea, driven and tossed by the wind; for the doubter, being double-minded and unstable in every way, must not expect to receive anything from the Lord. (Jas 1:6-8, NRSVCE)
Hail Mary...

Glory be...

Decade 3

Our Father

No one can please God without faith, for whoever comes to God must have faith that God exists and rewards those who seek him. (Heb 11:6, GNT)
Hail Mary...

Jesus said to her, "Did I not tell you that if you believed, you would see the glory of God?" (Jn 11:40)
Hail Mary...

If you had faith even as small as a mustard seed, you could say to this mountain, 'Move from here to there,' and it would move. Nothing would be impossible. (Matt 17:20, NLT)
Hail Mary...

I will look towards the Lord. I will wait for God, my Savior. My God will hear me. (Mic 7:7)
Hail Mary...

Truly, I say to you, whoever says to this mountain, 'Be taken up and cast into the sea,' and does not doubt in his heart, but believes that what he says will come to pass, it will be done for him. (Mrk 11:23, RSVCE)
Hail Mary...

I can do all things through him who strengthens me. (Phil 4:13, NRSVCE)
Hail Mary…

This is the boldness we have in him, that if we ask anything according to his will, he hears us. (1 Jn 5:14, NRSVCE)
Hail Mary…

If we know that he hears us in whatever we ask, we know that we have obtained the requests made of him. (1 Jn 5:15, NRSVCE)
Hail Mary…

I waited patiently for the Lord's help; then he listened to me and heard my cry. (Ps 40:1, GNT)
Hail Mary…

Rejoice in hope, be patient in suffering, persevere in prayer. (Rom 12:12, NRSVCE)
Hail Mary…

Glory Be…

Decade 4

Our Father…

He is near to those who call to him, who call to him with sincerity. He supplies the needs of those who honor him; he hears their cries and saves them. (Ps 145:18-19, GNT)
Hail Mary…

Whatever we shall request of him, we shall receive from him. For we keep his commandments, and we do the things that are pleasing in his sight. (1 Jn 3:22)
Hail Mary…

Whenever two of you on earth agree about anything you pray for, it will be done for you by my Father in heaven. For where two or three come together in my name, I am there with them. (Matt 18:19-20, GNT)
Hail Mary…

Listen to my voice in the morning, Lord. Each morning I bring my requests to you and wait expectantly. (Ps 5:3, NLT)
Hail Mary…

In my distress I cried out to the Lord; yes, I prayed to my God for help. He heard me from his sanctuary; my cry to him reached his ears. (Ps 18:6, NLT)
Hail Mary...

You did not choose me but I chose you. And I appointed you to go and bear fruit, fruit that will last, so that the Father will give you whatever you ask him in my name. (Jn 15:16, NRSVCE)
Hail Mary...

You do not have what you want because you do not ask God for it. And when you ask, you do not receive it, because your motives are bad; you ask for things to use for your own pleasures. (Jas 4:2-3, GNT)
Hail Mary...

I will do whatever you ask in my name, so that the Father may be glorified in the Son. If in my name you ask me for anything, I will do it. (Jn 14:13-14, NRSVCE)
Hail Mary...

In distress you called, and I delivered you; I answered you in the secret place of thunder. (Ps 81:7, RSVCE)
Hail Mary...

You love him, although you have not seen him, and you believe in him, although you do not now see him. So you rejoice with a great and glorious joy which words cannot express, because you are receiving the salvation of your souls, which is the purpose of your faith in him. (1 Pet 1:8-9, GNT)
Hail Mary...Glory Be...

Decade 5

Our Father...

For one believes with the heart and so is justified, and one confesses with the mouth and so is saved. (Rom 10:10, NRSVCE)
Hail Mary...

I keep praying to you, Lord, hoping this time you will show me favor. In your unfailing love, O God, answer my prayer with your sure salvation. (Ps 69:13, NLT)
Hail Mary...

Jesus told them, "I tell you the truth, if you have faith and don't doubt, you can do things like this and much more. You can even say to this mountain, 'May you be lifted up and thrown into the sea,' and it will happen." (Matt 21:21, NLT)
Hail Mary...

Whatever you ask for in prayer with faith, you will receive. (Matt 21:22, NRSVCE)
Hail Mary...

Faith is the substance of things hoped for, the evidence of things not apparent. (Heb 11:1)
Hail Mary...

But you, beloved, build yourselves up on your most holy faith; pray in the Holy Spirit. (Jude 1:20, RSVCE)
Hail Mary...

Look with favor upon the prayer of your servant, and on his supplication, O Lord my God, and so that you may hear the prayers which your servant pours out before you. (2 Chron 6:19)
Hail Mary...

We know that God does not listen to sinners; he does listen to people who respect him and do what he wants them to do. (Jn 9:31, GNT)
Hail Mary...

The Father will give you whatever you ask of him in my name. Until now you have not asked for anything in my name; ask and you will receive, so that your happiness may be complete. (Jn 16:23-24, GNT)
Hail Mary...

Thus therefore shall you pray: Our Father who art in heaven, hallowed be thy name. Thy kingdom come. Thy will be done on earth as it is in heaven. Give us this day our daily bread. And forgive us our debts, as we also forgive our debtors. And lead us not into temptation. But deliver us from evil. Amen. (Matt 6:9-13, DRA)
Hail Mary...

Glory Be...

Abbreviation

Gen-Genesis
Exo-Exodus
Lev-Leviticus
Num-Numbers
Deut-Deuteronomy
Josh-Joshua
Judg-Judges
Ruth-Ruth
1 Sam-1 Samuel
2 Sam-2 Samuel
1 Kgs-1 Kings
2 Kgs-2 Kings
1 Chron-1 Chronicles
2 Chron-2 Chronicles
Ezr-Ezra
Neh-Nehemiah
Tob-Tobith
Judith-Judith
Est-Esther
1 Mac-1 Maccabees
2 Mac-2 Maccabees
Job-Job
Ps-Psalms
Pro-Proverbs
Eccl-Ecclesiastes

Song-Song of Solomon
Wis-Wisdom
Sir-Sirach
Is- Isaiah
Jer-Jeremiah
Lam-Lamentations
Bar-Baruch
Eze-Ezekiel
Dan-Daniel
Hos-Hosea
Joel-Joel
Amos-Amos
Obad-Obadiah
Jon-Jonah
Mic-Micah
Nah-Nahum
Hab-Habakkuk
Zeph-Zephaniah
Hag-Haggai
Zech-Zechariah
Mal-Malachi
Matt-Matthew
Mrk-Mark
Luk-Luke

Jn-John
Acts-Acts
Rom-Romans
1 Cor-1 Corinthians
2 Cor-2 Corinthians
Gal-Galatians
Eph-Ephesians
Phil-Philippians
Col-Colossians
Tit-Titus
Phlm-Philemon
1 Thes-1 Thessalonians
2 Thes-2 Thessalonians
1 Tim- 1Timothy
2 Tim-2 Timothy
Heb-Hebrew
Jas-James
1 Pet-1 Peter
2 Pet-2 Peter
1 Jn- 1 John
2 Jn- 2 John
3 Jn- 3 John
Jude-Jude
Rev-Revelation

More Titles from Gifted Books and Media

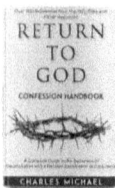

RETURN TO GOD
Confession Handbook

PREACHER'S HANDBOOK

**GOD'S PROMISES AND BLESSINGS
FOR AN ABUNDANT LIFE**

**FREEDOM FROM PORN
AND MASTURBATION**

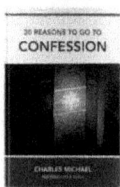

30 REASONS TO GO TO CONFESSION

EXAMINATION OF CONSCIENCE
For Teens

EUCHARISTIC ADORATION
*Prayers, Devotions, and
Meditations*

EXAMINATION OF CONSCIENCE
For Adults

**SCRIPTURAL STATIONS
OF THE CROSS**

GODLY CHILD
*Children's Guide to
Catholic Living*

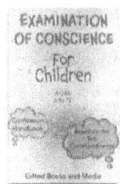

EXAMINATION OF CONSCIENCE
For Children

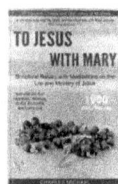

TO JESUS WITH MARY
*Scriptural Rosary on the Life and
Ministry of Jesus*

Now on Sale
Available in Paperback and Ebook
www.giftedbookstore.com

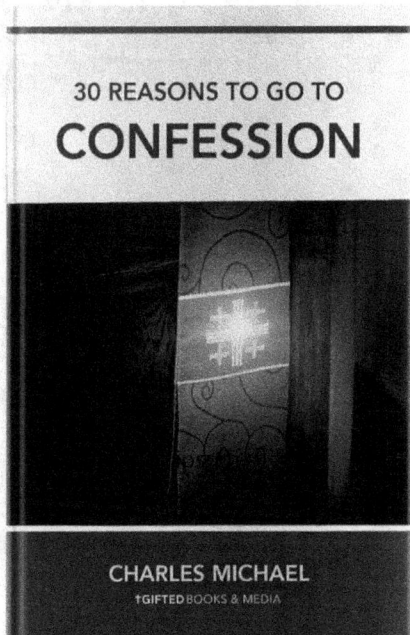

30 REASONS TO GO TO
CONFESSION

Now on Sale
Available in Paperback and Ebook
www.giftedbookstore.com

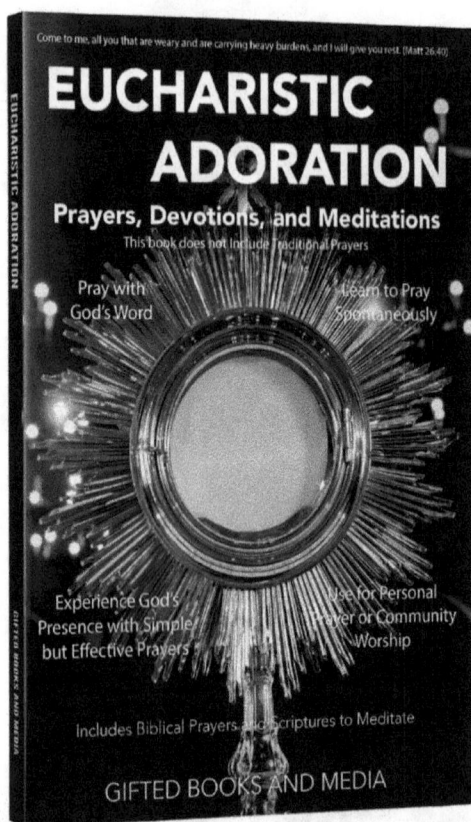

Come to me, all you that are weary and are carrying heavy burdens, and I will give you rest. [Matt 26.40]

EUCHARISTIC ADORATION

Prayers, Devotions, and Meditations

This book does not include Traditional Prayers

Pray with God's Word

Learn to Pray Spontaneously

Experience God's Presence with Simple but Effective Prayers

Use for Personal Prayer or Community Worship

Includes Biblical Prayers and Scriptures to Meditate

GIFTED BOOKS AND MEDIA

EUCHARISTIC ADORATION

Prayers, Devotions, and Meditations

Includes Biblical Prayers and Scriptures to Meditate

This Book does not include Traditional Prayers

Now on Sale
Available in Paperback and Ebook
www.giftedbookstore.com

www.ingramcontent.com/pod-product-compliance
Lightning Source LLC
Chambersburg PA
CBHW050132280326
41933CB00010B/1342

* 9 781947 343047 *